CRITICAL PLAYS

To My Brother-
in-Quine Joe -
Lots of love
+ looking forward
to more adventures
x ?
Anne
Chicago
2015

Social Fictions Series

Series Editor
Patricia Leavy
USA

The *Social Fictions* series emerges out of the arts-based research movement. The series includes full-length fiction books that are informed by social research but written in a literary/artistic form (novels, plays, and short story collections). Believing there is much to learn through fiction, the series only includes works written entirely in the literary medium adapted. Each book includes an academic introduction that explains the research and teaching that informs the book as well as how the book can be used in college courses. The books are underscored with social science or other scholarly perspectives and intended to be relevant to the lives of college students—to tap into important issues in the unique ways that artistic or literary forms can.

Please email queries to pleavy7@aol.com

Critical Plays

Embodied Research for Social Change

By

Anne Harris
Monash University, Australia

and

Christine Sinclair
University of Melbourne, Australia

SENSE PUBLISHERS
ROTTERDAM / BOSTON / TAIPEI

A C.I.P. record for this book is available from the Library of Congress.

ISBN 978-94-6209-753-7 (paperback)
ISBN 978-94-6209-754-4 (hardback)
ISBN 978-94-6209-755-1 (e-book)

Published by: Sense Publishers,
P.O. Box 21858, 3001 AW Rotterdam, The Netherlands
https://www.sensepublishers.com/

Printed on acid-free paper

PRAISE FOR CRITICAL PLAYS

The rapidly expanding community of art-based research seeking models for inquiry together with those in the arts, education, psychology, social relations, and all fields concerned with how the creative process can further human understanding will welcome *Critical Plays* by Anne Harris and Christine Sinclair. Long before we started deliberating the nature of legitimate research methods, theatre and enactment plumbed the depths of human experience, generating lasting evidence of how fiction and drama have unique abilities to articulate and embody the complexities and subtle realities of the personal psyche, human relationships, and social action. It is time to integrate the parallel play between the arts and other academic disciplines for the benefit of all.

> **– Shaun McNiff, author of *Art as Research* (2013) and *Art-Based Research* (1998), and University Professor, Lesley University, Cambridge, MA (USA)**

Critical Plays: Embodied Research for Social Change is one of the most methodologically creative and theoretically innovative sources to date for arts-based research. Using autoethnographic writing strategies to create deeply embodied characters, this play-as-research-text moves the reader into the critically reflexive felt-sense experience of students and professors engaging qualitative research and critical pedagogy for social change. Scholarly, performative, and creative, *Critical Plays* is a necessary text for the multidisciplinary qualitative research classroom.

> **– Tami Spry,** *Body, Paper, Stage: Writing and Performing Autoethnography*

Harris and Sinclair bring not just their expertise as arts-based researchers but their *artistic quality* to this exceptional book. The characters' monologue and dialogue are genuine, insightful, and unabashedly honest.

> **– Johnny Saldaña, Professor Emeritus, Arizona State University (USA)**

True to the precedents set in the Social Fictions Series so far, in *Critical Plays* Harris and Sinclair offer a bold experiment researching principles of arts-based research in scripted form. Drawing on their experience and inquiry as scholars and artists, the authors set their play in a graduate level methods class – a clever backdrop for exploring their understandings of the complexities of arts-based research through the multiple perspectives and various investments of their characters. With the integrity of using a performance-based method for traversing this rich and provocative research-scape, this book will undoubtedly prove an invaluable resource for scholars, instructors and students of arts-based research ... as well as an engaging and sophisticated read!!

> **– Diane Conrad, Assoc Professor of Drama & Theatre, University of Alberta (CAN)**

Critical Plays takes you inside arts-based research on a visceral, pedagogical, and artistic level. The authors share a fictional classroom narrative in the form of a playscript, exploring the dynamics and complexities of working in an arts-based way. Highly engaging, deeply informed, and artistically rendered, I strongly recommend this book for both the newly initiated and highly experienced arts-based researcher. A must read.

> **– George Belliveau, Professor, University of British Columbia (CAN)**

Critical Plays: Embodied Research for Social Change is an important addition to the field of arts-based research. The original and innovative approach undertaken by Harris and Sinclair is used to explore the research journeys of university students and their teachers by presenting their reflections, interpretations and reactions through this play text which examines significant elements of arts-based research through this process. The humanity and authenticity of each character engages and resonates with the reader. Characters directly address the audience allowing co-construction and counterpoints of reflection throughout the research journey. The transformative value and strength of arts-based research is presented in an aesthetically-crafted play (research text) which provides insights into the complexity of this field for those who seek to embody this approach. Each scene centres on an important aspect of arts-based research and provides the reader with greater understanding of this approach and where it is positioned in the field of qualitative research. Harris and Sinclair's passionate advocacy of arts-based research underpins this text which is enriched by their extensive experience and expertise in the arts field. This is an engaging, thoughtful, and significant text which is a 'must have' on any bookshelf.

– **Margaret Baguley, Associate Professor of Arts Education, University of Southern Queensland (AUS)**

This new book is an engaging and innovative addition to the scholarly literature on arts based and arts informed research methodologies. Written with insight, humour and deep knowledge of the field this performance text explores both the potential and power of creative research approaches. A must for emerging and experienced qualitative researchers.

– **Robyn Ewing, Professor of Teacher Education and the Arts, University of Sydney (Australia)**

To paraphrase the Bard, 'Plays are such stuff that reality is based upon on and our lives are awaken by their insights'. Such is the work of Harris and Sinclair. Be prepare to LOL as you 'conspire' or 'breathe with' (Barone) the script recalling many class events, reflecting upon why things are this way, and challenged to change your behavior as students and teachers. As both researchers and playwrights, they have compiled a fiction that is all too real. Can't wait to see it performed!

– **Joe Norris, Professor of Dramatic Arts, Brock University (CAN)**

"The point here is that knowing is a multiple state of affairs, not a singular one. In pragmatic terms knowing is about relationships."
Elliot Eisner, 2008

Vale Elliot Eisner, March 10, 1933-January 10, 2014

TABLE OF CONTENTS

ACKNOWLEDGEMENTS

Christine and Anne would first of all together like to publicly thank Patricia Leavy for her support, enthusiasm, and ongoing commitment to arts-based research and researchers around the globe. In a contemporary context, Patricia is doing perhaps more than anyone to advance the cause and diversity of ABR in scholarly fields, and is its most vocal public advocate – and for this we are immensely grateful. As a series editor, she is creative, passionate and collaborative – who could ask for more? We extend this professional gratitude to our publisher, Peter de Liefde, production assistant extraordinaire Bernice Kelly, and to Sense Publishers, for their bravery and commitment in publishing what many still regard as 'risky' texts or those lacking in rigour, and for these repeated leaps of faith, we are most grateful. We extend our collective thanks too, to the many colleagues, collaborators (both scholarly and artistic), students, friends and research participants whose voices have directly and indirectly helped create these composite characters, and deepened our own understandings of the power and reach of arts-based research. On a more personal note, Anne would like to thank Christine for her steadfast commitment to the scholarship of both embodied and theoretical research, a road harder to travel in these neoliberal times; the text you see here reflects only a small snapshot of our collaboration and of Christine's ongoing 'life well-lived' in creative scholarly enquiry, and I continue to be privileged to be the beneficiary of that knowledge for which I am always grateful. I would also like to acknowledge Achol Baroch, Julianne Moss and Joanne O'Mara at Deakin University, Mary Ann Hunter at University of Tasmania, Enza Gandolfo and Greg Curran at Victoria University, Clare Hall, Geraldine Burke, and the whole *Arts, Creativity and Education* research group at Monash University – all of whom continue to provide me with a rich and critical home for continuing this work; and lastly to Ruth Redden for her love, and own creative input and never-ending patience in these demanding and emotional journeys. Christine would like to thank Anne, firstly for inviting her on this remarkable road trip, and then for taking her somewhere new; and, for the questing spirit and tireless intellectual and creative energy that she brought to all the conversations, deliberations and drafts and redrafts that kept us company along the way. The future is bright and beckoning for such a talented and courageous exponent of ABR. Christine would also like to acknowledge the support and inspiration of her friends and colleagues in arts education at the MGSE and the many, many educators, artists, teachers and students who taught her well and kept the spark alive. And she would like to thank her family, for their tolerance and good humour and unconditional support for all these strange and wonderful adventures that make up an academic life. Finally, an acknowledgement to a muse on his passing: thanks to Elliot Eisner, to whom this book is dedicated, for showing us, among other things, that knowing really is a 'multiple state of affairs'.

INTRODUCTION

PROLOGUE

It's a Tuesday, about 6pm, the first night of a semester-long class in Arts-Based Research, and a small and eclectic group of students assemble in their somewhat shambolic tutorial room to begin the trek through topics as varied as 'truth and verisimilitude', 'Creative/ cognitive tensions', 'questions of representation', 'rigour' and 'ethics'. This fictional classroom is the site of our inquiry, and these characters the lens through which we examine and illuminate that inquiry into the nature of arts-based research as we understand it as scholars, and as we come to know it as artists.

CRITICAL FICTIONS

The arts deal with the evocative, the symbolic, and the expressive, with exploring through and communicating about experience in ways that transcend the verbal and the cognitive. The pliability of the arts to open doors to understanding has provided compelling argument for the exploration of creative and performative forms of expression in the transmission of research understandings and new contributions to knowledge. Through the *Social Fictions* series, Patricia Leavy continues this tradition, by creating new spaces for dialogue between arts-based researchers and those interested in or provoked by new sites and modes of inquiry.

Scholars are increasingly showing the diversity of methods and methodologies in approaching the work of doing arts-based research (see for example, Rolling 2010; Cahnmann-Taylor & Seigesmund, 2008; Knowles & Cole 2008; Barone & Eisner 2012; Leavy 2013). New approaches are emerging each day, and for this reason we are very pleased to be able to make a contribution to the rapid development of performance texts as arts-based research. The *Social Fictions* series is unique in its ability to trouble the lines between fiction and research, indeed fiction-as-research, taking arts-based research another step forward in its development and potential.

Our book locates itself in an educational context – through its setting in a fictional classroom and its central action as the teaching of an arts-based methods class. However, we aim to speak more broadly to the principles of ABR, addressing the opportunities and challenges encountered by those who create it and those who reference it in their own work. While our play is set in a classroom, its characters provide a conduit to a range of social research contexts. These characters, coming come from all walks of life and academic disciplines, bring those experiences into their own growing understanding of ABR, through which fundamental questions of ABR and its many contexts can be considered or tested. We see this book as a contribution to the expansion not only of arts-based research, but performance-based research as a sub-field, and the great diversity and potential yet to be fully explored here.

ABOUT THIS BOOK

In *Critical Plays*, as in other texts in this series, the fiction is embedded in the classes, interviews, collegial conversations, and creative collaborations we have both experienced in our work as arts-based researchers. Through the language of performance text, we embody our students, our participants, and ultimately ourselves in the characters of *Critical Plays*, and hope that the dialogic and performed basis of this inquiry brings to life some of the methodological conundrums that we ourselves have grappled with, and continue to grapple with.

This play of eight characters charts the difficult but rewarding journey for both students and teachers of arts-based research. Through a postgraduate-level methods class, these disparate characters discover a different side of themselves, while they discover a new side of academic research. As in life, the two lecturers – Barb and Kurt – do not escape the confronting nature of this work, and the undeniably (and sometimes painful) collaborative nature of it. Their journeys as individuals, as collaborators, and as researchers are intertwined. The text interrogates not only the 'doing' of contemporary research, but the 'why bother' or 'so what' of research as well. Returning research to its role as a deep and personal inquiry into the nature of life and the cosmos, these researchers find that arts-based inquiry both reflects and explodes the rules, traditions and ethics of conducting research for social change and inevitably, must come to terms with how this deep engagement with ABR within an institutional setting challenges and provokes them into their own acts of individual and social change.

As we ourselves – like these characters – embody social change through our work, *Critical Plays* was a collaborative project. Firstly, in our approach to the inquiry – playwriting as method – we were not only negotiating the artistic constructions of meaning on the page through the creation of character, action and plot, but also, playwright to playwright (researcher to researcher). The notion of multiple truths and multiple perspectives was played out through the act of writing itself. This required us to explore how we would write together, how we would inquire through the vehicle of the play, and how we would arrive at shared understandings. This brought a richness and complexity to the process of writing and to the research experience. After all, we come to this work from very different perspectives – professional playwright and ABR scholar; theatre director and performance ethnographer – resulting in contrasting approaches to research and playwriting. Ultimately we found that the most effective way for us to write together, was to write separately and to share our understandings of the project, of our inquiry, of our characters and the play, through the artefact itself. Our co-construction of meanings emerged, just as it does in Boal's Image Theatre work (1995), through a version of 'silent negotiation', with the artwork as the site of the embodied discourse. By working this way, we were able to *show* each other what we meant, artistically, through the work, as well as by talking about it. This was a powerful tool and we suspect a useful one for other collaborative creative researchers.

INFORMING THEORY

We've drawn on a range of theoretical and research traditions as we have developed this work. We note the historical influence of qualitative researchers such as Conquergood (2002), Eisner (2008) and Denzin (2003), who forged the argument for research practices which were "grounded in active, intimate, hands-on participation and personal connection: 'knowing how' and 'knowing who'" (Conquergood, 1991:196). Such practices, they suggested, generated a more dialogic approach to research, allowing for the possibility that understanding could be achieved through highly contextualized symbolic, emotional or affective engagement with new knowledge, as well as with the more accepted propositional knowledge garnered from "empirical observation and critical analysis from a distanced perspective" (Conquergood, 1991:196). It is against this backdrop that the seminal figures in arts-based research – Conquergood (2002) and Madison (2005) in performance ethnography; Barone and Eisner (2012), and Cole and Knowles (2008) and McNiff (2013) in arts-based research – provided theoretical building blocks upon which works including *Critical Plays* have been made. As Barone and Eisner (2012) observe, the processes of selection, refinement and focus that are intrinsic to the construction of a literary/artistic form, also serve the researcher in pursuing a line of inquiry. Importantly, the artistic form allows for nuance and the spaces between events and characters to speak, and to reflect deeper understandings that cannot be captured only in words.

Performed research has qualities which distinguish it from other text-based forms, for example, the embodied, the live, the visceral, and the symbolic representations of what Eisner describes as "ineffable knowledge" (2008:5). These qualities critically influence the ways in which researchers, performers, participants and audiences engage with the experience of seeing the work or reading the performance text as an artwork.

Tami Spry (2011) has developed performative arts-based inquiry further by bringing autoethnographic practices together with performance ethnography. She describes her approach in which "a critical stance of the performing body constitutes a praxis of evidence and analysis. We offer our performing body as raw data of a critical cultural story" (p 19). Spry's sense of the performing body as data informs our own embodied practice, as playwrights inscribing lived experience in the characters we create, characters who will further come to life in performances based on this playscript. This is the strength of arts-based research: its ability to breathe and enact on multiple levels and in multi-disciplines at once, an embodiment both

4

individual and collective, which constitutes by its intersubjectivity an epistemology and a lived experience of social change.

PERFORMANCE TEXT AS RESEARCH/ PLAYWRITING AS RESEARCH

What makes this text research and not just a play? Artists have long asserted our own systematic approaches to our work as equally rigorous, but including an affective dimension only strengthens its worth as new knowledge. Artists have always aimed to reflect, critique and extend society's understandings of ourselves as individuals and collectivities. Similarly, so have qualitative researchers. If we consider that the writing of the play is an act of inquiry (playwriting as method) then we can begin to see embodiment itself as methodology, a system of thought and set of tools.

Through the artform, in this case the writing of the play, we identified a line of inquiry – a quest for a new understanding, new knowledge. And in the construction of the play we continued this inquiry. The play, once crafted, provided a site of inquiry and then too an artistic, informed representation of that inquiry. Through the writing of the play script, we sought to clarify our understandings of specific aspects of ABR (topics for different classes in our fictional ABR methods class) and the process of clarification was conducted through artistic and conceptual problem-posing, and at times problem-solving; for example, how do we understand ethical issues for the arts-based researcher in a rich, rather than a simplistic way, and subsequently represent them so that others can understand or experience these ideas?

In this questioning comes the political potential of ABR to not only reflect society, but help transform it – something artists have long acknowledged. The idea that art can be made with no attention to the culture in which it is shown, on which it comments, and for whom it is created, would be a strange notion to most artists. Socio-cultural considerations are at the heart of why artists do what they do. So too are they central to arts-based research, indeed perhaps more central to many of us than ontological or epistemological questions of methodology. This does not mean that ABR lacks rigour but rather that the social function – indeed the research potential for new knowledge but also new 'knowing' – of arts-based research speaks to more aspects of the human condition than simply the intellectual aspect. What ABR has to offer is only now emerging, and we hope here to make some contribution to that rising wave.

THE AUDIENCE

Through this text, our aim is to provide an experience that is artistic as well as a substantial encounter with research. The characters who populate it are drawn from our lived experiences as researchers, teachers, and performance makers. *Critical Plays* is to us the systematic study of a classroom culture, comprising of six students and their two teachers, imaginatively conceived from experience, observation, interviews, communicty consultation (thematic analysis, etc.), and shaped into performance text which can be enacted or read as a script/text.

Our audience for this book includes all qualitative researchers and students, not only those of arts-based research, but more broadly those who see the expansive potential of arts-as-research in and across multiple disciplines. One significant intention of modeling this ethnographically-informed performance text as research resides in its potential to be relevant to the lives of our research students, in reflecting their own experiences and in highlighting pathways that are increasingly open to them as they begin their own scholarly research undertakings and journeys in a new and rapidly-evolving global research landscape. Thus, the book will be useful in the context of courses that address research methods, pedagogy and curriculum, arts-informed research and those concerned with research ethics. In research courses or for those graduate students doing thesis work, we hope the book provides additional insights into the lives of research participants and students, and into the intensely emotional and sometimes confusing methodological and ethical conundra that often accompany these journeys.

In addition, the book addresses themes and issues relevant to students of communications, ethnography across disciplines, rhetoric, education and the sociology of education, drama and theatre arts. As such the book invites interrogation of critical ideas and insights afforded by the active, imaginative engagement with the fictional characters and their 'real' research dilemmas and challenges. Lastly, we share the hope that this text and the play within it can be read or performed purely for pleasure by any interested readers or actors, as Leavy has articulated as a goal for her first book in this series, *Low-Fat Love* (2011).

In creating *Critical Plays*, we have used both formal interviews and our own experiences rendered through diaries, emails, brainstorms, free-writing sessions and dialogue together throughout this process. We have used the triumphs and detritus of our everyday lives – as artists do, as teachers do, as researchers do – to inform the protagonists Barb and Kurt, and to imbue them with the repetition of heartbreak and grinding demoralization that scholarly work in neoliberal times can sometimes seem to generate. Equally, we use the humanity of the characters in this work to remind students of the great need and political power of retaining emotion and relationality in the research space, an act of supreme social action as we see it. Arts-based methods as seen in this play and the entire Social Fictions series we hope remind readers of the great and urgent need to continue creating new "methodologies of the heart" (Pelias 2008), and disseminating this work widely. In this way we can remain scholarly activists, not just in participant communities 'of difference', but in our own fractured, sometimes very fragile worlds.

REFERENCES

Barone, T. & Eisner, E. (2012). *Arts based research.* Thousand Oaks, CA: Sage.

Boal, A. (2000). *Theatre of the oppressed* (new edition). London: Pluto Press.

Cahnmann-Taylor, M., & Seigesmund, R. (2008). *Arts-based research in education: Foundations for practice.* NY: Routledge.

Conquergood, D. (1991). Rethinking ethnography: Towards a critical cultural politics. *Communication Monographs, 58*(3), 179-194.

Conquergood, D. (2002). Performance studies: Interventions and radical research. *The Drama Review, 46*(2) (T174), Summer, 145-156.

Denzin, N. K. (2003). *Performance ethnography: Critical pedagogy and the politics of culture.* Thousand Oaks, CA: Sage.

Eisner, E. (2008). Art and knowledge. In J. Gary Knowles & A. Cole (Eds.), *Handbook of the arts in qualitative research* (pp. 3-12). Los Angeles, CA: Sage.

Knowles, G., & Cole, A. (2008). *Handbook of the arts in qualitative research: Perspectives, methodologies, examples and issues.* Thousand Oaks, CA: Sage.

Leavy, P. (2009). *Method meets art: Arts-based research practice.* New York, NY: Guilford Press.

Leavy, P. (2011). *Low-fat love.* Rotterdam: Sense.

Leavy, P. (2013). *Fiction as research practice: Short stories, novellas, and novels.* Walnut Creek, CA: Left Coast Press.

Madison, S. D. (2005). *Critical ethnography: Method, ethics, and performance.* Thousand Oaks, CA: Sage.

McNiff, S. (2013). *Art as research.* London/Chicago: University of Chicago Press.

Pelias, R. J. (2008). *A methodology of the heart: Evoking academic and daily life.* Walnut Creek, CA: Rowman/Alta Mira.

Saldaña, J. (2005). *Ethnodrama: An anthology of reality theatre.* Crossroads in Qualitative Inquiry Series, Vol. 5. Walnut Creek, CA: AltaMira Press.

Spry, T. (2011). *Body, paper, stage: Writing and performing autoethnography.* Walnut Creek, CA: Left Coast Press.

CAST OF CHARACTERS AND SETTING

Barb Grattan (professor) – early 50s, energetic, always moving, attentive but a bit nervous. She is knowledgeable about this place and these systems, and despite her nerves her confidence shows through. She has a warm voice and face that belies her relentless concern with procedure.

Kurt Smith-Whiteley (lecturer) – late 30s, looks like a hippie, would not pick him as an academic apart from the uber-cool expensive leather satchel he carries. He is ruggedly attractive and relaxed in his presentation style, and his voice somehow conveys his jazz musician identity.

Francine Nebbins (student) – 23, Honours Arts student in Performance Studies. Planning on researching Australian women playwrights of the 20th Century – from communism to feminism, but is not clear how she will go about her research or where she hopes it will take her career-wise. She is unsure about her future. Her research models are Holly Hughes, Peggy Phelan and other performance studies scholars- practitioners.

Andrea Schuck (student) – 43, primary school generalist classroom teacher doing her Masters. Andrea is creative and chaotic, wanting to do something 'different' in her research so that she can take it back to her school. Doesn't know what she wants to do exactly, but wants to change the culture of her school through her research. Not a confident student, possibly choosing ABR to avoid writing. Research focus: Shakespeare in the primary classroom. Her research models include Jonothan Neelands, George Belliveau and Elliot Eisner.

Gerard Posniak (student) – 46, School Principal, enrolled in the Doctor of Education in Educational Leadership, he is an ABR sceptic and is taking the class as a course work requirement only because it's the only one that fits in with his timetable. He has already mapped out his study, has a fully developed proposal, identified participants, planned for the survey, and is currently completing the ethics applications for the university and the department. His research models include Australian John Hattie and critical pedagogue Peter McLaren, but no ABR scholars.

Malcolm Rogers (student) – 58, is a near-retirement Professor of Nursing and Allied Health, and former head of a large community health centre in a low socio-economic region of Melbourne. He is also a professional jazz pianist, but has never brought this into his research at all. He has spent a lifetime as a quantitative researcher. He has done extensive research into grief and end-of-life care, but more from an institutional care and policy perspective. Lately, his faculty has had a lot of success using whole body prosthetics and role play for training pre-service nurses and health care aids, and obviously on a personal level he believes in the power of music and art therapy. He is not at all sceptical, yet he is brand new to ABR as a practitioner.

Ajak "Suzi" Deng (student) – 24, single mother of two. Arrived in Australia 7 years ago. Has had little formal education either prior to or since arriving in Australia, but very bright and ambitious. She attended 1 year of TAFE ESL classes, then has intermittently tried to study real estate and acting. The arts are her great love. She wanted to be the first Black woman on Australian television, and even did a video audition but didn't get in. She has been in a number of plays in town, but often her childcare needs interrupt her ability to commit. She has now gained portfolio entry to Social Work and has taken this class because she thought she could do an arts project, but she is feeling very intimidated. Her research model is Tami Spry because she is a passionate performer.

Jaime Rebeck (student) – 32, is Kurt's PhD student who doesn't turn up until Week 6 – she is a powerful voice from the 'field'. Anthropology student currently in the central Australian desert researching Indigenous filmmaking using an ethnocinematic approach, Jaime is in constant online contact with Kurt but is not

10

contributing to the class the way she should be. She is struggling with common ABR issues such as ethics, intercultural complexities, remote research locations, power imbalances, and boundaries with her supervisor Kurt, on whom she may have a crush. Conducting her research in an aboriginal community in the Northern Territory, Jaime continually confronts these and other challenges associated with transcultural arts-based research as a different way of knowing, in a community that isn't her own. Her research models are Trinh T. Minh-ha and Linda Tuhiwai-Smith.

SETTING

This play is set mainly in an Australian urban university classroom in which an (evening) arts-based research methods class takes place throughout the action of the play. It is a fairly old-school room, with little except an overhead projector, a data projector, desks and chairs.

There is a screen at the front which is used throughout, sometimes as a classroom projection screen and sometimes as a device of the play.

Some action of the play also takes place in other minimally-defined spaces such as: the two lecturers' homes, their offices, a cafe, a public housing meeting room, and a street. These spaces do not require sets for production, but rather screen projections and sound may be used to set the scenes, and minimal props can indicate the spaces.

PROLOGUE

KURT

Is in his office. It is (perhaps surprisingly?) very ordered – doesn't necessarily match his free and easy look. There are artefacts – gifts and treasured artworks from his time in remote communities and Laos where he lived for some time. There is also a framed arthouse photo of a younger Kurt performing in front of a crowd of adoring fans. Kurt is playing the saxophone, trying to improvise but it's not working. He keeps trying a lick and loses the groove, starts again. He begins to check his watch, knowing he is going to be late for class.

BARB

Is in her office which is full of papers and photos – a seminal trip to Scotland of many years earlier, some of her paintings, her kids and her husband Dougie. There are production photos, and stacks of paper and folders fill the room, the furniture, etc. She is pacing.
I don't know why I do this to myself … *every … time!*
I'm a fraud. I just feel like a … complete fraud. Why did I think this was a good idea? Why did I think it was a good idea to co-teach with an inexperienced teacher something like an arts-based research class that is going to take my *whole* heart and soul? Could I not just have picked a statistical methods class or something? Jeez ….
(she emails Kurt)
Dear Kurt, I still have not received your lesson plan for tonight and class is looming. Any ideas?
(she hits send, and simultaneously we hear the 'ping' on Kurt's email of it arriving. He doesn't notice, as he plays right through it.
Beat.
She picks up the phone, dials. His phone begins to ring. He stops playing, stares at the phones, starts playing again. She hangs up, frustrated.)
Oh great!
(they both check their watches again, and rush out)

SCENE / CLASS 1: SUBJECTIVITIES

(A small junky classroom with a dozen chairs with fitted half/desk tops. An old whiteboard, with the remains of many notes from previous classes not quite fully erased. There is a large clock on the wall. Six o'clock is showing, though it's unclear whether this is the correct time or if the clock is working at all. The room is empty, but the sounds of people can be heard outside the door. A young woman, about 23, enters.)

FRANCINE
(checks clock, then her watch) Six o'clock. Really? I'm never early.
(to audience) I'm never early. I like things to be underway in a class before I arrive. That way I get the vibe of the class but don't have to contribute to it, except by coming late. And you can tell a lot about a lecturer by the way they react to you when you interrupt them. I once withdrew from a class after the first week cause the artic stare I got when I walked in chilled me to my marrow – that was a woman without compassion – no way I'd get an extension from her without extreme measures. It was a no brainer, I got out of that class as soon as I could. Luckily I came across Kurt and he had me hooked. He was giving a lunchtime lecture on jazz as research, but really he was wooing every woman there – the smile, the stories, the deprecating humour. Talk about charisma. I would have over-enrolled just to be in his class. I didn't realize there'd be two of them running this. Hey, what if the woman's a real ice maiden. Now that would be, I don't know, ironic? Anyway, I already know what I'm going to do in my research. I've known for ages, since before the summer break. I had my research question weeks ago – maybe I'll keep that to myself for a while, though – let them think they inspired me to formulate something fresh – one of the tricks of the trade for a professional student – this is my fifth year here. But I've said too much, I don't even know you. Now here I am, first person in the room and I'll have to choose a seat before anyone else – that's an unfamiliar experience.

(Francine tries many seats before finding one that she thinks allows her minimum exposure. She's just settling in with iPad and headphones as Kurt enters with other students Malcolm, Gerard, Andrea and Francine together, chatting happily.

Moments later, Barb arrives, and starts to arrange printed materials on the small front desk, then attempts to fire up the computer in order to operate the data projector sitting next to an antiquated overhead projector. Kurt and Barb move the overhead projector onto the floor. While the students look around for suitable seating, Barb & Kurt huddle over the computer and the data projector, attempting unsuccessfully to bring it to life.)

ANDREA
(to audience, as she finds and organizes several chairs into a semicircle) People say you always know if there's a teacher in the room because they've rearranged the chairs. They might be right. I wonder if there's a research question in that? I'm hoping this is a talkative lot because I haven't got a clue what we're supposed to be doing tonight – I know I'm supposed to have a research question ready to hand in or, share or some such thing. I've got five questions and I'm pretty sure they all suck. And Gerard's here – he was my old boss before he got the nod to run the P-12 – I'll tell you this much for nothing, he'll have his question neatly typed and placed in a manila folder with copies for everyone in the class. A-type personalities as school principals. I wonder if that's a good research question? *(pulls several pieces of paper out of her handbag)* I had a brainwave in the car on the way here, wrote it down at the traffic lights. That's the one I'm going to read out if I'm asked – if I can find which one it is. God I hope we get a break for a coffee. I came straight from school and had yard duty at lunch time. I haven't sat down since 11 o'clock this morning and I was up at 6 to get the kids off to school – not that I'm complaining. I hate whingers. *(she sits)*

GERARD
It's already 6.10. Clearly, the technology doesn't work. I have 2 hours of emails waiting for me when I get home so I really hope this class finishes early tonight. I've prepared my research question

and have made copies to distribute, which should expedite the discussion of my question to get things started. As all good leaders know, any plan is better than no plan and I'm presuming that this IS the plan for tonight's class – group discussion and, I hope, a quick sign off on the question so I can continue with the project I've mapped out. They still can't get the technology working – I'm not entirely pleased.

(The students have seated themselves in the semicircle and are waiting for some kind of cue from the lecturers. There is an awkward pause as the students watch the lecturers struggle with the technology. Kurt realises they are waiting on him.)

KURT
Introduce yourselves please. Take a few minutes to get acquainted. We'll be starting soon, promise.

(There's a slight pause as the students look at each other, wondering who's going to begin.)

MALCOLM
I'll start – 'age before beauty'. Hi, I'm Malcolm.

ANDREA
And I'm Andrea, hello. I'm a bit nervous. Oh, and this is Gerard, we know each other already, don't we Gerard?

GERARD
As you've heard already, my name is Gerard. Hello Andrea, how are you. Oh, and it's Gerard, not Gerry.

(They all look expectantly at Francine, who still has her headphones on.)

FRANCINE
(Without pulling her earphones out.)
Hi, Francine

MALCOLM
(to Suzi)
And what about you, what's your name?

SUZI
My name is Ajak, but please call me Suzi – it's easier for … it's easier.

MALCOLM
Hi Suzi. Welcome.

KURT
Just a few minutes more and we'll be all sorted. Sorry you guys – this room isn't used too often and the cabling is ancient.

(They continue struggling with it under the following)

MALCOLM
I can't believe how small this group is. I thought this class would be really popular. I've watched arts-based research gain steady hold in health and medicine – and to great effect, too – but I've never really tried it myself. It feels good to be a student again. And only thirty years after my last studies – things have certainly changed. Except for that overhead projector there. I think that was in use in the last methods class I did. Applied statistical methods in allied health – circa 1985 – Yes, I think they were cranking up that old faithful back then. I remember being blown away one night when a lecturer took out a pen and wrote on one of the transparencies, **while we were watching**. That was about as arts-based as things got back then. And here I am tonight, another methods class, and there's going to be music and painting and performance. I'm in research heaven.

SUZI
I think this might be a mistake. Kurt made it sound so great and so easy, to come along to his class, but I'm just starting out. Some of these people are old, way older than me. They must have done a lot

of study. Research is a scary word – I'm not sure how it fits in with my Social Work course, but Kurt seemed to think it would be something I could use and something I'd be good at. He must know, right. He's got a doctorate and he's the teacher. He must know what he's doing. As long as I don't have to say anything I'll be ok. So that's a plan, right? I'll sit here next to the girl with the headphones and not say anything til I've got an idea of what's going on. Yep, that sounds like a plan.

(Finally, the title slide for the class appears on screen)

(Kurt takes 'centre stage' with laser pointer in hand to begin the class. Barb moves to the side, presiding over the course materials to be handed out later. She watches. Kurt leads the students through his slide show, in silhouette, without sound.)	Welcome Arts-Based Research Methods: An introduction Your MCs: Kurt and Barb
As the class progresses, Barb stands to the side, attentive, presiding over the materials to be handed out, and waiting for her turn. She addresses the audience directly, talking to herself aloud.	The self-conscious aim of life is to find expression, and art offers it certain beautiful forms through which it may realise that energy. (Oscar Wilde)
BARB I still feel like a fraud. Or the class monitor. In a moment he'll stop speaking and it'll be my turn and I'll get to distribute the handouts and talk about the assessment. Suck it up sweetheart. This was your choice. Kurt thinks they've put me here to keep an eye on the new boy, just in case he strays too far from the flock. Not so. I offered, no teaching load, and not much glory. I wanted to be there.	• What is the line of inquiry? • How does method inform practice; and how does practice inform method? • How is this work communicated to honour the artistic/creative practice; to honour the voices of participants? • How is this work communicated in the academy– as new knowledge and as credible research? • How does methodology support this inquiry?

Thought I could help. Be a mentor to the young star. We should all take our turn in the mentor role, that's what I've always believed. But I was being disingenuous. I wanted to be in the proximity of passion. And this is what it feels like. Like fraud. And the worst part about it, he, that young boy, he thinks I'm a fraud as well. What would she know about arts-based research? What would she know about art? I listen to him speak. He's poetry in motion. Oh damn, I think that's a cliché.	Your work should: make an original contribution to knowledge in terms of the originality of the approach and/or findings.
	Denzin says: The seventh moment … is concerned with moral discourse, with the development of sacred textualities. The seventh moment asks that the social sciences and the humanities become sites for critical conversations about democracy, race, gender, class, nation-states, globalisation, freedom and community (2003:9).
I just didn't anticipate finding myself quite so … at odds, so marginalized. It was a crazy thing to do, to offer to co-teach this course. I am not an artist. I'm an academic, a serious researcher with a track record. And my workload really is unforgiving. Hell, I *want* this ABR class to thrive, which he doesn't realise. I want to learn more about it too, that's part of the hook for me. I desperately miss *learning*, I even wish sometimes I could be a student again. What a beautiful luxury that is. But co-teaching a new class like this is probably as close as I'll get – I've been reading for weeks now already, all the key authors – the Barone and Eisner, Saldana, Leavy, Ardra's work, all the Denzin forays into ABR. It's the – what is it that's so tantalizing when I see Kurt in full flight, reading his stories, introducing his latest work in music, or in applied video – what is it? – ethnocinema. It's the ineffable … the blessed relief of the unknown knowledge – that which is known but cannot be spoken, he just seems to embody it – was I ever like that?	

KURT *(Briefly heard from the shadows)* This work aligns itself with the arts-based research tradition about which Elliot Eisner and Tom Barone have written extensively and modelled so eloquently in their own research writing. They identify seven features of Arts-Based Research:	
(As each of the seven features are highlighted there is a mimed discussion amongst the class. It is animated and all the students are involved, except for Suzi, who sits apart.) BARB The creation of a virtual reality and as he turns in my direction, I know he expects me to not understand, but of course I understand. I've got a fucking doctorate, even if it was on parchment – I have to stop doing that … I'm not that old. Of course I understand the creation of the virtual world, the construction of a fictional framing in which the imagined becomes 'real' or is given the appearance of the real, the verisimilitude which permits the authentic voice to be heard. As for ambiguity, well, ABR is at the heart of ambiguity – to revel in the partial and contradictory truths that co-exist – in scholarly worlds, in virtual worlds … in all worlds, let's be honest.	Seven Features of Arts-Based Educational Inquiry. 1. The Creation of a Virtual Reality. 2. The Presence of Ambiguity. 3. The Use of Expressive Language. 4. The Use of Contextualised and Vernacular Language. 5. The Promotion of Empathy. 6. Personal Signature of the Researcher/Writer. 7. The Presence of Aesthetic Form.
Yes, it's the ineffable that brought me here, Kurt.	As Michael Polanyi says, we know more than we can tell. Thus, not only does knowledge come in different forms, the forms of its creation differ. The idea of ineffable knowledge is not an oxymoron (Eisner, 2008:5).

(The focus reverses. Barb is now in silhouette and Kurt takes up her position in the light.)

KURT

Great discussion. I'm going to hand over to Barb now who's going to talk you through the hard stuff – the nuts and bolts of things, assessment, deadlines, you get the picture. Barb?

(Kurt watches briefly as Barb begins her Powerpoint then pulls his phone out of his pocket on which he reads an email to himself, as)

KURT	BARB'S POWERPOINT
"Hey Kurt, I'm not going to be coming to the class. I've enrolled and will send you updates, but I'm into the most important part of my study and I can't get away. I'll do the assessments and I'll even make it back for the presentations in the last week – should have a shitload of footage by then. Jaime". (pause)	IEX 904 Arts-Based Research Methods: An introduction ASSESSMENT REQUIREMENTS Journal: Hurdle requirement – weekly. Submission Date – 2 weeks after last class Proposal: Draft –Submission Date Week 3 Weekly tutorial presentations Research Presentation: includes revised draft, rationale for ABR, work sample
Why do I always feel like she's the supervisor and I'm the doctoral student? And why does that shit me instead of making me feel happy that she's at least self-motivated? (beat) Because she's a pain in the ass, that's why.	**Further information on the Journal** **A reflexive journal:** i.e. (of a method or theory in the social sciences) taking account of itself or of the effect of the personality or presence of the researcher on what is being investigated. *Reflexivity: is the process of examining both oneself as researcher, and the research relationship. Self-searching involves examining one's "conceptual baggage", one's assumptions and preconceptions, and how these affect research decisions, particularly, the selection and wording of questions. Reflecting on the research relationship involves examining one's relationship to the respondent, and how the relationship dynamics affect responses to questions*

	For next week: **Journal entry** on ABR Epistemologies: Knowing and Feeling **Five minute tutorial presentation** about your research proposal – "What I know and what I feel"

(Kurt breaks in, rudely interrupting Barb mid-sentence)

KURT
Folks, there is one other student in this class – Jaime Stenock – who is doing a PhD with me in ethnocinema. She is based in Alice Springs, and is making collaborative videos with Indigenous young people about the music scene in Central Australia. The study is really pretty ground-breaking, I must say, even though Jaime herself isn't Indigenous, but –

SUZI
– A culture vulture?

KURT
Excuse me?

SUZI
Culture vulture! That's what we call white people who come in and – you know, want to research all the natives. That kind of thing. No offense.

KURT
Uh, yeah. Okay. Well keeping it specific and avoiding *generalisations*, let me just reassure you that Jaime is, well, she's not like that – I mean, she's –

BARB
(saves him)
This is so perfect – I love when this happens!

KURT
Sorry?

BARB
That kind of ethical dilemma about working cross-culturally, or working in new methods or alternative media – that is so what ABR is about, right Kurt? These are cutting edge approaches, and *of course* issues of ethics and power are always present. I think this is a great place to pick it up next week.

KURT
(Comes to)
What? Oh yeah exactly, great job everyone. That's it for this week. Sorry we didn't get time for a coffee break. Bring your coffee mugs next week and we'll bring the biscuits. We'll make sure we take a break – get some time for chatting – that's when the real thinking happens, isn't it Barb?

GERARD
(Raises hand)
Excuse me? Didn't you ask us to bring our research questions for sharing? I mean, some of us came prepared and I'm not sure why we haven't covered this. Does that mean we can go ahead and proceed with our planned project?

(Barb passive aggressively looks to Kurt to handle this.)

KURT
Yeah sorry about that – the time just got away from us. Bring them back next week – Gerry, right?

GERARD
I prefer Gerard.

KURT
Yeah cool – Gerard – bring them back next week and we'll pick it up there.

24

(Gerard is not pleased but holds further complaint for now.)

KURT
Okay, and finally: to start you off on your reflexive journals, which – as we said online is absolutely crucial to this process – please consider the statement "I'm walking out the door and I'm thinking about …" right now, class #1 – get it down, ok? Let's document this process right from the beginning.

Okay, thanks everybody – see you next week.

(Kurt and Barb leave, Barb reassuring him quietly.

As the students are packing up their things, chatting amongst themselves, sending and checking text messages, each one pauses briefly and addresses the audience directly)

FRANCINE
I'm walking out the door and I'm thinking about the crush I had on my first year History lecturer. He was so smart, so aloof, so revealing. I followed him around, not exactly literally – took every class he offered, made sure I was in his tute group, read everything he wrote. It was unrequited but I did discover the Australian communist playwrights of the 30s and I fell in love with them instead.
(she leaves)

GERARD
I'm walking out the door and I'm thinking that it's March and I need to have my study designed and completely calibrated by the end of May. That's not a problem, I've just about wrapped up the design, now just waiting on some guidance with my ethics. It would help if I had a supervisor lined up. And I'm deeply sceptical – Kurt is, well, a jazz musician who seems to think of himself more of a rock star, and strikes me as completely unqualified to be guiding me through my methods study, as minimal as my needs are. And I think he has an agenda.

(he leaves)

ANDREA
(holding a scrap of paper in her hand) I'm walking out the door and I'm thinking that Elliot Eisner is a revelation. What does he say? *(she reads)* "The quest for certainty, as Dewey points out, is hopeless" [4]. No, that's not the one, it's this one *(finds another piece of paper)*: "Words, except when they are used artistically, are proxies for direct experience. They point us in a direction in which we can undergo what the words purport to reveal. Words, in this sense, are like cues to guide us on a journey" [5]. God, I love TS Elliot. I'm always struggling to find the right words – the best proxies – for my experiences with the children. It's as if I **know** what needs to be said, what needs to be discovered, but I just can't find the right words or put them in the right order. I'm getting onto Book Depository tonight – gotta get that Eisner book. Better get the Dewey one as well.
(she leaves)

MALCOLM
So Kurt spent time in the central desert – I wouldn't have taken him for an outback kind of guy. More like a pretty boy who can do no wrong. Harmless enough, but not used to failure. And what kind of good research can you do if you're not used to failure? Okay Mr Teacher-Man: I'm walking out the door and thinking – I'm thinking about not thinking too much at all. Don't go there Malcolm. Just keep it light, stay in the moment. One day at a time.
(he leaves)

SUZI
I'm walking out the door and I'm thinking, next week I'm coming with a dictionary, or, maybe, I'm not coming at all. When is a Sudanese gonna research a white person? Never, cuz we don't care!

FRANCINE
(returning)
Hey, Suzi, I think I might live somewhere out your way. Would you like a ride?

SUZI

No thanks. I'd rather wait 20 minutes for the train, then walk a kilometre home from the station in the dark, thanks anyway.

(Beat)

Kidding. That'd be great, thanks.

(Francine laughs and they leave together.)

SCENE / CLASS 2:
COGNITIVE / CREATIVE TENSIONS, OR WHAT I KNOW VERSUS WHAT I FEEL

(Gerard is alone in the tutorial room, setting up his Powerpoint presentation, as ANDREA comes in.)

ANDREA
Hi Gerard, what's that?

GERARD
Hi Andrea. I'm just setting up my presentation for tonight – I want to make sure this antiquated technology works, after last week's stuffing around.

ANDREA
Yeah, that makes sense. What a waste of time, eh?

GERARD
(flicking through his)
Yes, very frustrating.

WEEK TWO
METHODS CLASS

FIVE MINUTE PRESENTATION
GERARD D. SMITH

RESEARCH QUESTION

Principals as executives: business based models of school leadership in public primary education

ANDREA *(taking note)* Wow, this looks great! You've done so much already. GERARD I just want them to sign me off so I can get going – hmm – where's that slide that was up when I came in?	**METHODS** 1. Mixed method approach 2. Questionnaire (state-wide) – primary data gathering instrument 3. Semi-structured interviews – Principals, Deputy Principals, School Administrators, School Council Presidents 4. Document review – Policy documents 2000-2013 **DISCUSSION** This thesis builds on and contributes to work on the strategic role of educational leaders, and particularly public primary school principals. Although some in the field (Bell, 2002; Forde, Hobby, & Lees, 2000; Kelly, 2005) have questioned the utility of strategy as a concept, particularly with its ties to economics, marketing and capitalist ventures, there has not been an explicit research focus of what strategy means in educational leadership. As such, this thesis provides additional insight by taking stock, assessing and integrating the existing body of literature on strategic leadership and management in schools and by going beyond what is already known and setting forth new frameworks, perspectives and researchable questions. **(Ref: Scott Eacott –Ph.D abstract)** **ANY QUESTIONS?** Thank You.

(puts up slide) ANDREA Dunno. I did a Powerpoint – well I did several, and I brought a handout for everyone – do you think that's too much? I'll show you the handout (she looks for it as he seems completely disinterested in her.) GERARD There it is – one of the lecturers must have set it up earlier. Strange they're not here. Probably slipped off for a latte or a quick vino before class. Do academics drink chardonnay any more? Probably pinot grigio. No, it'd be a red. ANDREA (laughing) So true! Shiraz no doubt! (Gerard actually joins her in a laugh as Kurt enters.)	**Arts-Based Research Methods: An introduction** **Welcome to Week Two:** The empirical and the affective – What I *know* versus what I *feel*

GERARD
Good evening, Kurt.

KURT
Hey Gerard – right, Gerard?! Ha! I got it right this time. Week 2 – not bad. And …

ANDREA
Andrea.

KURT
Sorry –

ANDREA
That's fine.

(The other students file in, greeting one another. Barb rushes in with a stack of handouts and sits, still working on her laptop.)

KURT
Okay everybody, can you give me a hand clearing the room? We are going to start with a game tonight –

GERARD
Smashing –

(Andrea laughs out loud)

KURT
– that requires you to find a partner. Gerard and Andrea, looks like you have already found each other so why don't we shake it up – Andrea and Malcolm? Gerard, you get me. Francine and Suzi, I guess that leaves you.

(They pair up as they all move the furniture aside)

KURT
Barb – you sure you don't want to play?

BARB
(drily)
Uneven numbers, what a shame.

KURT
Okey doke. So what I want you to do is tell your partner a couple of things about yourself: one thing you **know** and one thing you **feel**. Okay everybody, and: three, two, one … GO!

(General loud GROANS, but then all three pairs begin simultaneously, but we then hear snatches of each conversation as the focus moves backwards and forwards amongst the pairs.)

KURT
(To Gerard)
Well, I'm Kurt, of course, and one thing I know about myself … apart from lots of reading, I don't prepare for my classes, I see them as extended improvisations and, one thing I feel … Sad when I'm working at my computer on glorious spring Saturdays …. *(pause)* your turn.
(pause)
One thing you know and one thing you feel – about yourself. Give it a go.

GERARD
I'm Gerard and I know … I derive a great sense of satisfaction from alphabetising my vintage vinyl collection.

KURT
Not categorized – jazz, rock, funk? Just in alphabetical order? Really?

FRANCINE
(To Suzi)
Hi I'm Francine and you're Suzi, I know that already. What do I know? Um, well my birthday is November 14th! That's dumb. Anyway, what do I feel – I love the feeling of starting something new. New horizons, the unexpected, that's what I love about research. Ok, I've told you something I know – the date of my birth – and something I feel – I have a researcher's heart … tell me something about you. I think I did all the talking when we drove home last week. Anything you like.

AJAK/SUZI
I'll tell you about my nickname. My name is Ajak but people call me Suzi. Suzi is not too white, is it? There's a lot of Sudanese girls

called Suzi. Basically Ajak is too hard for white people to pronounce or to remember. This is one thing I know: white people have bad memories. But one thing I feel? I don't know –

FRANCINE
Well, how do you feel when white people keep getting your name wrong, or forgetting it?

SUZI
That's probably the least bad thing white people do. If you want to know what I feel.

MALCOLM
(To Andrea)
... So I just kind of fell into this latest research interest. It seemed like a logical progression from the last big project I did scoping policy in end-of-life care. There just seemed to be so much more to be learned by digging down into the human experience. I think nurses are much more likely to connect with that than they are with that great 3 volume policy document that every Allied health agency has sitting on their CEO's shelf, or propping open the door to the tea room. But I'm monopolizing the conversation, what about you? I know you're a teacher and you have two children and a very busy husband, but what do you really know?

ANDREA
I know I'm absolutely terrified about the presentation I have to give in a few minutes. And there's empirical evidence – fourteen drafts of the powerpoint slides between last week and this morning. Let me tell you something I feel at the same time as I'm terrified. Excited. I love being here. This is amazing. I get to talk to some big wig professor and he's one of my classmates, and I get to think about what things really mean, and how feeling and knowing are just different facets of the same multi-dimensional force.

KURT

That's remarkable Gerard. I had no idea you could use Dewey decimal for a home audio library and there's an app for it. I might check it out. Hey, we have to wrap up now. (*to all*) Thanks everybody, let's move on. The five minute presentations. Andrea's agreed to go first. Let's get this room in some sort of order so we can begin. Do you have a powerpoint presentation, Andrea?

ANDREA

Several.

(The students return chairs and tables to the middle of the room, and Kurt helps Andrea set up her Powerpoint. Simultaneously, Barb is working on her laptop, speaking aloud as she reads, looking up occasionally to acknowledge Kurt and the students as they move around her to re-set the room, mostly ignoring her.)

BARB

(To the class in general)

Here it is, our starting point for tonight's class: Epistemology

(reads) noun: Philosophy

The theory of knowledge, especially with regard to its methods, validity, and scope. Epistemology is the investigation of what distinguishes justified belief from opinion.

Derivatives: **epistemological** (adjective), **epistemologically** (adverb), **epistemologist** (noun) – ooh, I like that – *epistemologist*.

Origin: mid 19th century, from Greek *epistēmē* '*knowledge*', from *epistasthai* '*know, know how to do*'.

This is the time in any methods class where I love to engage students in a challenging, rigorous discussion about theories of knowledge. The debates we have. Questions like 'Is knowledge provisional or absolute?': an oldie but a goodie, anyone? Any thoughts? When starting a new unit I like to introduce students to the Greek roots of the word. Who knows the difference between epistemology and and etiology? Anyone? (*awkward pause, the students are not really attending to Barb at all, but preparing for their presentations*).

(to audience) I have to spend a great deal of energy trying to separate students from the ideas they're in love with: 'isn't that an opinion?' I ask. How does that constitute 'knowledge'. 'Because it's true', they'll say. 'Ah, truth', I say, 'truth is next week's topic'. How many years have I been doing this? More than I care to admit. And to be honest sometimes I have to ask myself if I'm any more certain of the answers now than I was when I started, but that's another discussion for later.

KURT
Barb, who are talking to?

BARB
(ignoring him, to all) Now, who do we have up first. Andrea? Thanks for starting us off. Tell us about your project – just a five minute overview is fine.

ANDREA

(Slide 1) This is Gretel. She's nine. She has been diagnosed with a learning difficulty. She hates coming to school. She loves art. She and her sister are currently in foster care as her mother is ill. She's in my Grade 3 class.	*Slide 1: Gretel*
So, what I know. To begin with a moment, from the classroom. A moment of surprise, uncertainty, what is it that	

Zimbardo calls it? Disruption. (I love that all my 'friends' from last semester's Research Survey course keep popping up when I write).

This is what I know:

I'm in the art room with the Year 3s. All term we have been looking at the Australian impressionists. What can we learn about Australia from the paintings of Tom Roberts and McCubbin and Streeton. I love these painters. I love the tactile encounter with oil on canvas – brushstrokes layering on heat and dust and grey gums – with that European sensibility lurking.

It's the hour before lunch and it's hot in the portable where our art room has been relocated while the new building is under construction. You can hear the cicadas outside. The children are restless. They're tired of the Australia story. You can see it in the way they lean into each other and sigh, as I start on the McCubbin tryptich, *The Pioneer*.

One of my very favourite works. **My** favourite works. I ask them what they see. We make a game of it. They spark up as the list of colours, shapes, sounds grows on the white board. How can you see sounds, Mrs Taylor? I wait. Gretel, always listening, never putting her hand up, puts her hand up. Cicadas Miss. I see cicadas.

Slide 2: Australian landscape

I gesture to the children, we walk to the windows, and open them wide. The cicadas roar. The children look upwards to the towering gums, to the late summer, to the world outside the classroom. I bend down, to see what they see. One by one, they walk back to the electronic whiteboard where I have the painting on display. I close the windows, grateful that we have windows, that our school is almost in the bush and that I can see what they see. Quickly, I replace the pencils I'd planned for them to use today, with my newly minted supply of watercolours.	*Slide 3:* 
I ask them to paint what they hear, what they feel. I pick up a brush and paint alongside them. (Oh that's just a picture of me when I was their age, painting, always painting) Is this what I feel, or what I know?	

And then we go outside … Beautiful isn't it? Can you hear the cicadas?	
This is what I think my project is going to be about – the angle of repose – perhaps more than that, perhaps its not just about how we look, but how we listen. Anyway, I'm still working it out. Thanks	My project is … the angle of repose and the art of listening

FRANCINE
I'll go next.
(Francine starts to set up)

KURT
Thanks Andrea, that was amazing.

BARB
Can you give us a little more detail please on your ideas for the outcome? What will this project look like, or consist of, if you know?

ANDREA
I think it'll be a multimedia exhibition – Grade 3s and their older siblings at the school. The work will be paintings, in the style of the famous Heidelberg School (Art Movement) and sound recordings,

39

made in our school ground and in the dry creek bed, and compositions inspired by the recordings. I will work with the children as they create the work, and record them and the work, over time, throughout the year.

KURT
That's beautiful Andrea. What are you most interested in about this study, do you think right now?

ANDREA
Well I guess the questions that keep going around in my head are, as teachers and artists and human beings: What are we looking at, where do we look from, what do we hear when we look. Do you know who I am from looking at what I am looking at? From seeing me through the eyes of my sibling? My teacher? Things like that – probably sounds ridiculous but –

BARB
Not at all, that's great. But do you have a central kind of research question for your project yet? You may **not,** which is fine – I'm just asking –

ANDREA
I've had a lot of questions already, but dropped most of them. The one that is sticking at the moment is exploring: *Shifting identities in the primary school classroom, art as mediator for children's multiple epistemologies.* Which isn't actually a question now that I say it out loud …

BARB
Okay thanks Andrea.

FRANCINE
I'm ready.

KURT
Okay Francine, take it away –!

FRANCINE

Enter, stage left, Dorothy Hewett, in a wheelchair, long faded blonde hair, bohemian scarf, and a cigarette, lighted, in a long ornate holder. That's my Dorothy. I've spent the summer reading all her plays and I feel that I know her already, but don't understand her at all. How could she call herself a feminist and allow herself to be abused by that man? That's a mystery. And why did she stop her autobiography at 1959? That's what I want to understand. The unreconstructed feminist who reconstructs her life, post communism. Here's a powerpoint presentation on what I know and what I feel. *(Francine flicks through her powerpoint presentation without comment)* Thanks very much. *(to audience, as Malcolm prepares to present)*	**Francine's talk** About knowing and feeling, not
	This is what I know… This is what I know?
	But in her web she still delights *To weave the mirror's magic sights;* *For often thro' the silent nights* *A funeral with plumes and lights* *And music, went to Camelot.*

SCENE / CLASS 2

	Dorothy
	This is what Dorothy knows *The stage is in darkness. A clap of thunder rolls away. Ushers in school uniforms and the rest of the cast take up their positions.* SALLY I rode forward through the blackened land. I found the forests burning and the fields wasted, waiting for rain. Upon a slope I saw a glimpse of light. Then I came to the Chapel Perilous.
	This is what I know Only questions ○ How could she call herself a feminist and allow herself to be abused by that man? ○ Are Sally Banner and Dorothy Hewett the same person? ○ How could she be in the communist party when they were all dominating misogynists? ○ And why did she stop her autobiography at 1959?
	My Project What I know for sure about my Honours thesis is the title. *The Empty Room, the unreconstructed life of Dorothy Hewett.*

	What I feel?
	How much time do you have?

FRANCINE
Oh god, sorry, how embarrassing.

KURT
No, that was great Francine. I can see there's a lot in there that is deeply personal to you, which is exactly where we start with arts-based research. Scary but spot-on.

FRANCINE
It's not scary, it's just a little annoying really –

MALCOLM
Good on you Francine. Beautiful thoughts. I always loved Dorothy and those other women of her generation. I think I might be up next. Is that ok Kurt?

KURT
Sure thing.

(*Malcolm begins to set up his presentation*)

BARB
Francine, if you'd like to speak more about how to make your own work in dialogue with Dorothy Hewett's, we can chat after class – I've been a big fan of her work all my life!

FRANCINE
To Barb

43

Thanks that was a nice try but I still feel like a complete idiot. How trite, how trite, what unbelievably reductionist crap that was. What is the point of these snapshot presentations anyway, without giving us enough time to do it properly? Maybe next time I should present on what I don't know, I'd have plenty to say on that. Oh, and I do have one more thing to add about what I feel. Maybe it's not knowledge, maybe it's an opinion. But, Kurt, why did you ask us to talk about feelings, I mean – why is that even relevant? Believe me, I could spend the entire semester talking about what I feel, but how is that even relevant? I hope this class is not going to be like this every week, laying our guts out on the table. I shouldn't have done Hewett – Those poems, you want to know how I feel? Like I **am** Sally Banner riding to the Chapel Perilous, before the fall … What I know for sure about my honours thesis is the title. *The Empty Room, the unreconstructed life of Dorothy Hewett.* And that's not changing.

(beat)

KURT
Okay, all food for thought, thanks Francine. Malcolm, you ready?

MALCOLM

Hi everybody. I'm Malcolm, as I think you all know now. And Francine, if you thought that was exposing for you, wait until you hear this! I might need some moral support after, but I'm going to give it a whirl – I tried to represent the five senses in this presentation, as they are central to my project, but PPT just shows me once again how un-sensual and un-creative it really is. Therefore I have resorted a 'traditional' layout for clarity's sake. But it's an interesting quandry, this question about knowledge. I wonder whether we should be replacing the noun with the	Week Two Methods Class: *Five Minute Presentation* Malcolm Rogers

verb, and making that our noun, knowing. What is my knowing? It's active, living, not a constant, not an entity, but, an engagement with life. Some of you know that I've been a nurse and lately have been stuck in administration running a large Allied Health Care centre down near Dandenong. In addition to that, most recently I've been hanging around these hallowed halls, you know, doing a bit of this and that, policy, research, teaching.

But two days a week, every week I work in a Palliative Care unit. Have done for quite a while now. That's where I go for my 'knowing'. When you spend time with someone in those very last days, you look in their eyes and you can just see … they're seeing something entirely different from what you see. And almost always, it seems to me, it is a period of moving from the 'what I know' to the 'what I feel'. What I mean is, people like me who have always relied on our brains, on intellectual certainties like doctors, academics, nerds like us – have to make a huge adjustment. Because as the body breaks down, which it must do for us all in the end, as the body breaks down the brain becomes LESS reliable, but the senses don't necessarily follow. In fact, in some ways what I've observed is that the senses become MORE RELIABLE, and the intellect less reliable. So this is why I really loved Kurt's question about knowing versus feeling, although the one challenge I would make is whether or not they have to be an either/or dichotomy. But I think this is exactly what arts-based research is all about, at least that's

What I know:
Palliative care

Life is short: effective end of life care is really an art.

Memory is sense-based: sight, sound, taste, smell, touch

What are we left with?

why I've taken this class – to find out. Anyway, here's my idea for a project *(talks to ppt)*	
SO this is my plan or approach for the project:	**Methods** • Interview 10 people with terminal diagnoses. • Interview 10 end-of-life carers (doctors, nurses, palliative care workers). • Let me and them all choose 1 artefact representing/requiring each of the 5 senses ad speak to that.
And here are the questions that are speaking to me at the moment.	**Research Questions** • How can arts-based research uniquely address my questions, feelings, and knowledge? • How can my research project be useful to others?
But because this is MY project, I also want to include some things I feel about stuff other than palliative care. When I'm not coming to work, you see, I belong to Kurt's tribe. I play a little piano. Jazz. I know a lot about feeling. About flow. About the senses activating as you start to go right off, fingers flying off the keys. So I know a lot about feeling but I don't think I can tell you about it. You'll have to come down to the Butterfly Club in the city in a couple of weeks – I've got a gig and that's when I can SHOW you something about feeling, Malcolm-style. Because to me that's the difference between arts-based and other research: in arts-based research	*What I feel:* • There is not a lot of great end-of-life care. • I want to do a project that provokes discussion and thought about this. • It must use as many senses as possible. • This is not based on research data but on my own gut feeling after working in this field for 30 years.

you SHOW rather than tell. It's embodied, it has to be felt. Don't you agree, Kurt? Barb?	
So, that's it for me. I'm just excited to be here, because when I discovered that it was possible to do research using all the senses, I said to myself. That's for me. I'm going to find out what that's all about. So that's my starting point. What's this all about?	The End Or rather ....The Beginning!

KURT
Thanks for that Malcolm, that sounds great. I think we'll hold discussions until next week, in the interest of time, ok? Gerard, you're already set up, right?

(GERARD hops up)

GERARD
Yes, I'm all ready –

KURT
Suzi, how would you feel about doing your presentation next week so we're not too rushed?

SUZI
That's TOTALLY fine – in fact, I don't have to do it at all –

KURT
Haha, no next week is great. You just get one week's reprieve. Over to you Gerry – Gerard! I meant Gerard –

(Gerard walks to the control panel with his handouts to begin his powerpoint.)

GERARD

Good evening and thank you for the opportunity to present my preliminary proposal. I have a handout here that you are welcome to refer to during my talk … I'm sorry. This is … absurd. Ridiculous. This just isn't …. No, I'm not doing this right now. I'm going to go. *(he leaves.)*

(Kurt follows him out as Barb stands to take the class back over. The following exchange takes place in the corridor simultaneous to the class dismissal.)

BARB

Okay well – we've done a lot. We have certainly got through a lot tonight, so –

SUZI

So me and Gerard will finish next week?

FRANCINE

And we'll get feedback, or – I mean, what was the point of this exactly if –?

KURT

Hey Gerard, what's going on? Something I should know about? You were all prepared. That wasn't exactly cool, leaving like that you know.

BARB

(To Francine)

It is to negotiate about your project, yes Francine. But more than that, it is intended to establish a safe space for sharing your work, a concept and a practice that is central to arts-based research. So we are modelling what we will be discussing as good arts-based research in this class. Is that okay?

FRANCINE

Sure I just –

SUZI
Let's go –
(*students all file out, staring at the conversation between Kurt and Gerard in the hall*).

GERARD
That's it in a nutshell: "Cool". I have no intention of being cool Kurt. I've done everything that's been asked. I've done the reading and prepared my presentation but I don't see anywhere where it says I have to be 'cool'. What a load of bullshit. Sitting watching those pretty powerpoints with pictures, and kids' art, and the senses, and how I 'feel'. It's none of your business how I feel. None. I will do the required work and yes, I'll attend class, but I will not be telling you how I feel and will definitely, most definitely not being coming to class to be cool. I will see you next week –

KURT
Come on Gerry –

GERARD
It's Gerard.

(He leaves as Barb emerges from classroom to see –)

KURT
Don't leave things like this. Let's talk this out –!

BARB
Well that looks like it went well. Shall we have a debrief before –

KURT
Sorry Barb, I've really gotta go.

(He leaves. End scene.)

INTERMEZZO 1: MISCOMMUNICATIONS

KURT is home, on the internet. He's messaging with JAIME, the absent student. In supertitles above the stage, we see the following dialogue:

JAIME
(to Kurt)
Hey groova!

KURT
(Irritated, writes)
Can we at least attempt to be professional in the way we address one another please?

JAIME
What would you prefer?

KURT
You're a smart person, think about it. How about doctor, just for something completely appropriate? Let's talk about your phd.

JAIME
I'm sick of it. I'd rather talk about you.

KURT
Well that's not how it works.

JAIME
Is this weird? I mean, is it just me or has it been weird?

(Kurt pauses, worried and over it. TOM calls in from OFFSTAGE):

TOM
Hey babe, are you eating?
(nothing)
Babe?

KURT
Yep, I'll be there in a sec.

(shake his head, writes)

KURT
Jaime, nothing's weird except that you still haven't finished your study and it's going on a year overdue now. What can I do to help you get to the finish line?

JAIME
I don't think you want to know what would help me.

KURT
I am seriously starting to be concerned.

(nothing)

KURT
Is there a problem Jaime? Because you have my full support but I do worry that you're getting a bit off track.

JAIME
I think you're getting sick of me.

KURT
I'm not sick of you. Please just think about what it is you need to move this thing forward. Why don't you sleep on it and let's talk tomorrow or Thursday.

JAIME
Can we Skype at least?

KURT
Ok.

JAIME
Thanks Kurt, *(smiley face)*. Night night, groova.

(End of message convo. He sits there, highly irritated but concerned. Not sure how to deal with this. TOM, from offstage)

TOM
Kurt, are you coming? I'm gonna start if you're not coming –

KURT
I'm coming – five minutes. Just have to check my email. There's one from Barb – I've gotta open it –won't be long, promise.

(projected in email format on the onstage screen)

–

Dear Kurt
Just thought I'd send off a quick email before the dust settles on the first couple of weeks. I have one or two thoughts I wanted to run by you before next week's class and we don't seem to have much time to chat between classes.

Firstly, congratulations on an excellent start to the semester. The class is small and this is a bit disappointing from a sustainability perspective. Nevertheless, it is an interesting, and diverse group. I guess time will tell whether it was wise to allow Ajak to take the class, given her inexperience in academic study. I did wonder if she was feeling a bit out of her depth so far? What was your take on her involvement tonight? She was very quiet.

There are some pedagogical issues at play with neophyte researchers – hence methodology units for postgrad students – and I suspect that they will require some attention during the semester. This is something we should work on together. We should address the question of collaboration for example. It's important of course, but can be tricky when assessment is involved.

That's the other issue I thought it might be useful to address early on, while there's still time to manage it. The assessment. The class presentations were an excellent idea and signalled to the students that they need to get cracking on their research. It'll put them on the spot, but in a good way. However, I did find the language of the assignments somewhat fuzzy. I'm coming to this unit with the presumption that you are wanting to demonstrate to the students (yes, and the university) that this is a credible pathway into and through research, and I support this intention. We need to be careful that the assignment doesn't appear too open-ended, as it plays to the stereotype of arts-based research as lacking in rigour. If we can't manage a well structured and clearly focused major assignment, with appropriate assessment criteria, how can we advocate for rigour?

And am I being presumptuous in assuming I will be involved in the assessing of the final projects? I don't want to find myself in the position of assessing the unassessable – I'm sure you don't either. I hope I haven't come across too strongly in my email. I am very much looking forward to how you approach epistemologies and affect over the coming weeks. Discussion of epistemology is one of my favourite topics in a methods class, so I will be standing by to put my two cents worth in.
Well done so far, and I'll see you next Tuesday.
Regards
Barb

KURT
What the fuck, Barb! So you're here to school me on ABR, is that it? Sure, let me do all the work, and you sit back and criticise … so passive aggressive, my god.
(begins to type)
Dear Barb …
Hi Barb …
Barb …
Why don't you take your condescending tone and your patronising manner and your epistemologies and shove them up your …

(he continues to type, but silently. He then pauses, reads back what he's written.)
Sleep on in Kurt, never email when you're angry – rule number one. Who told me that again?

TOM
(from offstage)
Babe! I've poured you a wine – come and get it!

KURT
That's who.
(He hits the delete button)
Coming.
(he packs up for dinner)
I just wish I could get my head around this job. I can't figure out the relationships, and I can't figure out the day to day. It's like there is nothing and everything to do, all at the same time. And like no one notices, but everyone sees everything, all at once too. It's crazy-making, I swear to god.

Sometimes, I wish I wasn't teaching at all. I wish someone would pay me to just research in music and performance and that would be it. Why is that so hard?! That's my gift isn't it – that's what I do that other people can't?

Research should be about the work. Not an abstraction, not a notion, not a theory about what life *should* be, but something to feed back into communities – work for social change, otherwise, what's the point? *Embodied* work for social change. That's what bugs me about this whole so-called scholarly scene – it's as if these guys don't even have bodies! Like everything doesn't always come back to the body. And I'm not talking about some ingénue with a crush who thinks I'm straight.

I feel like I can't fit in either world – on the one hand I've got academic overlords telling me all the time that what I do is not really research, rolling their eyes when I mention arts-based research, or critical creativity. You know what I feel like saying to them? I want to say 'so how is what you do seriously any more rigorous than my work? Try coming out into a community with a tape recorder and a saxophone sometime and see how easy that is. Try working with people *unlike* yourself for once, someone so different it hurts'.

And when I go out to run workshops with the kids, the whole community sector looks at me like I'm not to be trusted now that I'm in the room as a 'researcher musician' and not a 'community musician'. And I hate it, but I can kind of understand it at the same time. I had a Malaysian research assistant the other night tell me he would be the 'advocate' for the young people in our project. I was like 'what? Advocate for them?' and he was like 'yeah!' all smiles. I was like 'advocate to whom? Like, to whom are you advocating on their behalf?' And without skipping a beat he was like, 'To you!' like it was really great and I'd be so pleased or something. I'm like 'But why do you think they need an advocate with me? I mean, I'm here *collaborating* with them'. 'Well, you know' he says, 'I'm just here making sure they get represented fairly'.

And he didn't even see why that would cause me any grief at all. And then when I got offended he said he was really disappointed *in me!* For getting disappointed!
Jeeeeesus.
This job kills me, it really does.
beat.

TOM
(from offstage)
I'm finishing the bottle!

(KURT turns the light off and joins Tom for dinner, while the following email appears on the screen, with Kurt doing off stage V/O)

Dear Barb□
Firstly, thanks for your email. I'd like to take your lead in 'thinking

56

aloud' on email and open up a negotiation around what you see as your role in this class – so these are just ideas and I'm completely open to bounce back and negotiation – I think we have to accept some online dialogue this way due to our mutually busy schedules and so little funded planning time from the university – so thanks and I hope you take this in that spirit.

I'm so excited to be working with you as a collaborator, not as a supervisor – and I know that you have no interest in performing that role – you have certainly been there/done that for so many years I'm sure you're well and truly over it! So let's proceed from here as collaborators.

A few salient points which I'll try to keep brief:

– a thank you: for the many years and perspectives you bring to this material, it will really improve the unit – as your email demonstrates.

– a request: regarding your assessment concerns, I appreciate your offer and wonder if we might actually split up the work by allowing you the chance to run with a revision of my assessment – that would be great, and probably easy for you considering your very clear ideas about that.

– a suggestion: that we split up the running of the weeks equally, so we don't slide into an 'all Kurt' me-me-me show – which I know neither of us wants. I for one would welcome this shift, so thanks for opening that door. Next week before class perhaps we can find some time to split them up and then be able to learn from each other as we trade off.

– a provocation: I have a feeling, and it's just a feeling – that Suzi (Ajak) will actually be the heart and soul of this unit, and remind us all why we love ABR as much as we do – accessibility, after all, is at the centre of these approaches.

Many thanks again for your email, and I look forward to enabling you to have a more active input in the day-to-day working of the unit. If I think of anything before next week I'll be sure to send it on through. Thanks again Barb –□Cheers for now,
KURT

(end of scene)

SCENE / CLASS 3: TRUTH AND VERISIMILITUDE. 5:08PM

(Barb is sitting in the classroom ready for class. The students file in – Suzi and Francine together – Gerard alone, Andrea alone, and lastly Malcolm and Kurt together, laughing. Barb looks at her watch, annoyed. Malcolm and Kurt both notice her at the same time and freeze. Malcolm goes and sits down, Kurt goes to Barb.)

KURT
Hey Barb, sorry I'm late.

BARB
If you want me to open the class, that's fine. Just let me know in advance.

KURT
No, I just got talking with Malcolm and didn't realise the time.

BARB
If you could just call me if you're going to be late, that would be great. Thanks.

(Kurt puts his things down with a heavy sigh and takes a moment. Then:

KURT
Hey guys. Okay so last week we heard some amazing introductory thoughts on where you might each head with your own projects. Which brings us back to Gerard and Ajak, er, Suzi … sorry. Let's start with Suzi, shall we? Take it away Suzi.

(Everyone stares at Suzi.)

FRANCINE
She's not doing it.

KURT
What? Suzi?

SUZI
I didn't prepare anything, sorry.

(Dead silence. Gerard snorts in expected disgust, which Barb almost calls him on it, but realises she agrees and stares instead at Kurt, not intervening.)

KURT
Okay, that's cool. Gerard?

GERARD
No thanks, I'm fine.

KURT
Alright. Anyone want to say anything about last week?

(Long pause.)

MALCOLM
Well, I enjoyed it. It really opened my eyes to the range of things we could …. *(trails off)*.

FRANCINE
What if we tried to do some pair work? We could go off and do something and bring it back, as an exercise?

BARB
Thanks for the suggestion Francine, but in this kind of work –

SUZI
Yeah. What if we all did something together? To get to know each other better? As a group, or something? So we trust each other more. You know?

FRANCINE
Great! That's a great idea. Don't you think that's a great idea, Kurt?

GERARD
Oh Jesus.

KURT
What do the others think?

GERARD
I think I have paid a lot of money for this unit and I'd like to think there is some expertise in the room. Are we actually going to learn anything here?

FRANCINE
That's harsh Gerard. I think I've learned a lot already. Last week, for example –

ANDREA
Me too. I've been reading like crazy, and I'm thinking about this class all the time. Even when I'm with the Grade 2s, especially when I'm with the Grade 2s. I think a group task could work. I mean, my experience is only with primary students, but when we use collaborative arts practices with our students they really rise to the occasion. If they can do it, why not us?

GERARD
Except for the small fact that we're not primary school students.

FRANCINE
But the arts are embodied practices. This is an arts-based research methods class after all, Gerard, so—I think if you were expecting to sit around using powerpoints this was never going to be a good fit for you, if you don't mind my saying so.
In Performance Studies, you know, my background, we were pretty clear on *doing* as a way of knowing, of learning. I was taught that the

art *is* the theory and you can't actually do any form of practice-led research without actually doing stuff. So I'm in.

KURT
(looks at Barb who gives nothing away)
Okay. I can see there are a lot of different perspectives here. Francine is right that at the heart of ABR is the doing of a practice. The practice is the exploration. And the other core aspect of arts-based research is its ability to address issues of cultural and social significance, a particularly powerful tool for social change. And you're never going to change society by sitting in a room doing a powerpoint.

GERARD
You used a powerpoint.

BARB
You've got a point there Gerard –

KURT
(chooses to ignore this)
So I think we should give Suzi's suggestion a try –

BARB
I don't want to be a wet blanket Kurt, but this can't be for assessment. That's just how it goes here, you can't change the assessment after the class has started. As you know.

KURT
I'm not suggesting that. I'm saying we can do this as a preliminary exercise – it could be helpful as a formative task.

FRANCINE
Well I say yes! I'm all for Suzi's idea.

SUZI
(heartened by the support)

Well I just think you can't expect everyone like me to know how to do this shit, excuse the swearing. If you open this class to people like him [Malcolm] who run hospitals with all that education, and then people like me who don't have hardly anything then you have to help them. Otherwise it's not fair. If you're talking about social change and crap like that.

(Pause)

KURT
She's got a point there.

(everyone laughs, concurs, general support for Suzi. Gerard rolls his eyes and slumps.)

And Suzi, I want you to know that what is happening here – this renegotiation based on the needs of our group, as collaborators, as co-participants in a research journey – well that is *exactly* what the power of arts-based research is all about: knowledge, or knowing, as Malcolm described it, is not fixed, but co-constructed in collaboration. Our dialogue is a knowledge discourse as is our ACTION. So whether you get it or not, you have just ENACTED the principles of ABR right there. First in the class. You actually didn't TELL us tonight, but you SHOWED us. So thanks. For taking us to the next step.

MALCOLM
Well done Suzi!

GERARD
(mutters under his breath)
Shall we all join hands and sing Kumbaya now?

(beat)

KURT

Well Gerard it's interesting you should say that, because Kumbaya is a song with an ethnographic history that is very much about what we are doing here. Not to be too nerdy, but seeing as you brought it up: Kumbaya was a Creole song in the American South, a slave song that – like so many songs of this type – was stolen by a white man and claimed as his own. So a long history of ethnographers and linguists travelling the American South and other places trying to attribute these divers music traditions got completely erased by a more mobile, more affluent white man who just said 'it's mine' and everyone believed him. So thanks for bringing us back to tonight's topic: "Truth or verisilimitude in arts-based research". What is truth, and are we really concerned with it in academic research?

FRANCINE

Well if you're asking that as a legitimate question, I'd say I want to question what even is the truth, I mean does it even exist?

KURT

Nice one Francine! Truth or the appearance of truth? That in itself would be a great focus for a philosophy of research class maybe, in parallel with an arts-based class, wouldn't it? But for our purposes, I mean – to not get too far off track, let me say that I think we're all working toward our own truths here, and struggling to break through the verisimilitude. As put so well by Gerard, so thanks Gerard.

Now Suzi: any ideas on what shared activity you guys might do? We've only got about 2 and a half hours left. So we could spend an hour or hour and a half on an exercise, on the 'doing', in pairs, and then have a share back and discussion. What do people think?

(beat)

SUZI

You've been talking about truth. And that other word. I think we should do something truthful, or maybe I mean honest – I'm not sure what the difference is just yet.

KURT
Well as an exercise how about if we all go down the street and sit in a café and have a coffee. While we are there we watch and listen to everyone around us, and we make observations in a notebook –

SUZI
Or, what if? This is probably dumb but what if we can't take notes, we have to do it all by memory? For example, I'm not that good at taking notes very fast, but it might surprise you that I'm really good with memory and speaking. So this may be that I have an unfair advantage to this game, but if we did that, then we have to come back and act it out – **exactly** as we saw it. We each get one of the characters we saw, and then we come back and act it out with as many real lines as we can remember.

(dead silence. Everyone thinks it's amazingly cool, if a tiny bit terrifying, and are kind of stunned).

SUZI
No? Okay, well—

FRANCINE
No! It's fantastic! That is such a Performance Studies generative somatic exercise! I love it –

GERARD
I don't see what this has to do with –

MALCOLM
I love it. Gerard, maybe you and I can work together on this a little bit, to think about how it fits with your assessment task for the class.

GERARD
(they lock eyes. Gerard is annoyed, realising Malcolm is challenging him, but accepts the guidance and backs down)
Yeah, sure. Whatever.

SCENE / CLASS 3

ANDREA
I'll give it a try!

BARB
Kurt I think it's probably a good idea for you to go along with them isn't it?

KURT
To be honest Barb, I think we should step back, demonstrate some trust and let the group go without us. And we can stay here and do our development work on this class while they're doing theirs, if you think so.

BARB
If you think so.

KURT
Okay then. Well, what are the ground rules? Everyone agree with Suzi that there will be no writing, note-taking?

FRANCINE
Yep

ANDREA
No phones or devices!

KURT
Yep, good – everyone has to agree. Is that what you had in mind Suzi?

SUZI
Okay, no writing and no going off on your own. We have to stick together.

MALCOLM

Good idea Suzi. Let's stay as one group together, and rely on each other. But, we can speak to others outside of the group as part of the exercise, right?

FRANCINE

Yeah, great. Can we discuss what's happening analytically? Like ask questions or help each other?

ANDREA

No! We have to silently observe and remember.

GERARD

That's ridiculous. How will we know then if everyone's even got anything, or is just overwhelmed, or is just having a coffee and gazing into space.

FRANCINE

Meaningful eye contact.

GERARD

That's the limit! This is getting ridiculous.

FRANCINE

– kidding! I was just kidding Gerard.

KURT

(laughing) Okay, okay. It sounds pretty set. You all head down to Lygon Street – Malcolm, you'd know several places that would work well – some of the busier cafes or restaurants? And collectively pick a place that has enough people and conversations to choose from. You all sit together, and you have a drink or a nibble as a front for listening, observing and studying the people around you. Each of you chooses a person to inhabit, your 'character' to embody, and you tune into them particularly. You observe everything you possibly can about them – movements, tone of voice, looks, tics, what they eat, everything. You see how they interact with others – their

companions, the waiter, others in the restaurant – you are looking for the essence of the person – the truth of them. Then you come back here and we'll do some improvised work letting your characters come to life and then, maybe, interact. See if everyone knows who you are. Just like in music, it'll be an improvisation.

BARB
But Kurt, what if they all pick the same person?

SUZI
It doesn't matter, because we will see that everyone sees them differently. They might even seem like different characters to each of us. That will come out when we talk about it later.

FRANCINE
I think if the point is to spend some time together, and begin to practice embodied research, this is perfect. In fact maybe it's more perfect if there ARE overlaps in our choices, because it will point out how subjective ethnographic observation really is, and it will also make a point about what 'types' of people catch the researchers' eye. Don't you think Kurt?

KURT
There's more to it than that. It'll help you get to the bottom of tonight's topic – what are we looking at: truth or verisimilitude?

I think this is a perfect introductory practice-led activity and I want to thank Suzi for pushing us towards it. It's so cool you're in this class, I'm really glad.

(embarrassed, Suzi looks down and doesn't say anything).

FRANCINE
Totes! Me too Suzi.

KURT
Okay, off you go. See you in an hour.

(They all exit. For a minute, Kurt and Barb just sit there mulling.)

KURT
Really happy
Wow, that was soooo cool.

(pause)

BARB
I'm a bit nervous about the direction this is taking – was that even in your plan for tonight? Look Kurt, I know I've said this before, and you seem to have trouble believing it, but I'm your greatest champion. I've always been supportive of your work, and this unit would never have gotten up if it weren't for me taking it on over and above my workload. I do have a responsibility to the University though, to make sure everything goes smoothly, so I hope to god nothing goes wrong out there.

KURT
You know Barb, I actually DO have a PhD, which won the university medal for best thesis. So I don't think you need to worry too much. Maybe it's just that we have different approaches to the work, and you're finding it hard to be flexible. I know I have a lot to learn from you, but maybe – just maybe – you have something to learn from me too. The beauty of ABR is that it's rapidly evolving, so you don't have to exhaust yourself gatekeeping all the time. If everyone wasn't always disappointing you so badly, you might find you'd have more fun.

BARB
Take a flying leap Kurt.
(She walks out.)

KURT
This is going well so far.

(end of scene)

INTERMEZZO 2: DUSTING DOWN THE MUSE

(At BARB's dining room table at home – one end of the table cleared for eating, the other end has books all with a variety of sticky notes attached, computer open, a dissertation draft with sticky notes, a Saturday newspaper, some knitting needles stuck into a half completed sweater sleeve. Barb emerges from the kitchen with wine glass and opened bottle.)

Shit. Shit. That didn't go well. Bloody Kurt. Ok so I came on a bit strong. I better email him and apologise for the 'flying leap' comment. Hey Kurt, I've got an idea: stop pushing my buttons and I'll stop pushing yours. I really want this to work out. How good would it be to have a really solid ABR methods class running every year? Don't you get that, that's what I *want* – not to shut you down. Shit. We really should talk about this. I'll send him an email, ask him to come for coffee. I'll take him to Seven Seeds – or is that too bourgeois wanker for him? Ok, he can pick the place.
(beat)
I'm not a control freak, I just don't know where this is all going. It's only Week 3 for god's sake and already they're off doing performance ethnography in cafes.
(beat)
Ok so maybe I need to 'chillax' – yes, thanks Jono, tell your mother to take a deep breath. Tell you mother to stop talking to herself.
Ok.
Let me take a look at this schedule and see how we're splitting it up: Week Four is what? *Finding the form.* Oh and that's me he says. Great, I think. At least I'll get a chance to connect with the students. They probably think I'm the Class Monitor, or Kurt's RA! That's a bit harsh. It was good that they got to hear from Kurt – build some rapport so that they have a go-to person. That's what I'd do if I were leading this. But it's Kurt's gig, for now anyway. His vision, his passion.

What have I got to bring anyway? Listening to those students last week when they talked about their projects filled me with sadness.

Did I ever have a muse? Did I ever work with my heart as well as my head, find knowledge through feeling? Interrogate the cracks in the earth rather than the earth itself?

Once I did: that winter before Jono was born. Dougie and me in Scotland, listening to that music, going from Ceilidh to Ceilidh, gathering up the songs and the stories of the Highlands. I remember, sitting in the B&B, down in the living room, crackling fire, Dougie snoozing, and me with my notebook, writing. Not dry ethnographic field notes, those fleeting moments of story and poem, captured though images and dialogue. Maybe that was me stumbling over arts-based research? Where is that notebook? Probably in a box in the shed.

Those mountains were the muse. Looking out the window across the sea to Skye – not a cliché – just the view from my window. Grey squalls coming in off the sea and rolling up the hill to my window. And writing, beyond the fieldnotes, writing to my ancestors and to my children who'd never know the stories of their great-great grandparents, the tragedy of the Clearings.

If I'm really still, I can hear that music, feel that damp air rolling in, feel the scratching of the pen on the cheap notebook paper.
Where is that now Barb?
It's not Kurt's fault that it's gone. You let it roll over you, slide past the window. Twenty-five years later, it's in a box out in the shed.
(Beat)
Where's the torch. I might just have a quick look out there. See if there's anything worth sharing with the students next week. Maybe I'll start with narrative inquiry.
(She leaves)

(end of scene)

SCENE / CLASS 4: FINDING THE FORM

(Scene opens in the classroom, before class. Barb is working through her Powerpoint, somewhat agitated, making last minute changes. Francine arrives, carrying two take away cups of tea, stops at the door when she sees Barb. Checks her watch, is about to go out again, when Barb looks up.)

BARB
Hi. Francine? How's it going? Come in, I'm just doing some last minute tweaking on my Powerpoint slides. It's a kind of an academic nervous tic – can't seem to leave things be at the eleventh hour.

FRANCINE
I'm early. Again. Don't tell my parents: they think my lateness is a genetic aberration, I wouldn't want them to think I could control it. I … I actually came to meet up with Suzi. We thought there'd be no-one here. We just wanted to talk about this idea Suzi had.

BARB
Really? Do you want to run it by me? Don't mind me if I keep on with my tweaking. I can do two things at once.

FRANCINE
No, it's ok. It's Suzi's idea, not mine to talk about. We thought we'd run it by Kurt a bit later on tonight. What time will he be here?

BARB
Kurt's not in tonight. We're tag teaming now. Lucky you, it's all me tonight.
(beat)
Well if you don't mind, I might just get on with my prep. Here's the roll – could you sign in, and I'll leave you to it.

FRANCINE
Thanks (*she signs the paper and hands it back to Barb*). I might just wait for Suzi downstairs. She's late anyway. Must be having trouble

getting a baby sitter, or something. Thanks, Barb. I'll see you a bit later.
(she leaves)

(Barb continues her preparations. Gerard appears at the door)

GERARD
Evening Barbara. How are you? I understand you're taking this class tonight?

BARB
It's Barb, actually. I prefer Barb.

GERARD
Barb. Yes, good then. I understand that you'll be taking the class tonight, but I was wondering what time Kurt would be coming in?

BARB
Just me tonight Gerard. Lucky you. I'm just finishing off a few things before class. Here's the roll. Would you mind signing in?

GERARD
So Kurt isn't going to be here tonight? Oh, that's a bit disappointing.

BARB
You surprise me: after Week 2 I thought he might be off your Christmas list.

GERARD
It's not personal Barbara, Barb. We've exchanged a couple of emails this week and, well, frankly, Kurt's insight into my research design was really quite helpful. For a musician, he has a surprising grasp of statistics. Anyway, I had a couple of follow-up questions for him. I thought I'd catch him before things got underway.

BARB

Well perhaps you could run it past me in our break? I've been in this methodology caper for quite a while. I even did a stint with statistics back in the 90s. I could probably remember a thing or too.

GERARD

Thanks for the offer. I can probably manage via email. I don't really want to go through the whole preamble again – site, context, rationale, etc. – I've been through it all with Kurt. I thought he would have told you. After the … tense moments a couple of weeks back, Kurt got in touch with me. He invited me for a very nice coffee at Seven Seeds and we thrashed a few things out. He agreed not to continue challenging my methodology and I agreed to come back to class. Surprisingly good listener, Kurt.

BARB

Well you learn something new every day. Look, could you excuse me Gerard, I've just got a couple of last minute things to do with my lecture for tonight.
(as she is speaking, Malcolm and Andrea enter together, chatting)

MALCOLM

Hi Barb! A lecture tonight eh? That's an interesting approach to Arts-Based Research.

BARB

Of course it's not for the whole two hours. Just a few principles that I think might be important to our discussion.

MALCOLM

Ah, discussion as well.

BARB

Of course. I think discussion is essential. It's not all about the lecturers and what they know.

MALCOLM
Couldn't have said it better myself.

(*Students begin to organize the tables and chairs, still piled up against one wall, into a semi circle, facing Barb, Gerard passes roll on to Malcolm and Andrea. Suzi and Francine arrive, each carrying one of the cups. Suzi is talking.*)

SUZI
… Saturday afternoon. Come at about 2.30. The common room is on the ground floor, just near the playground. I think there should be about ten women. I've asked about 25 so far. Every time I go to the shops or the playgroup, I meet someone who I think might be interested and ask her to join the group. I think I can get some money from the council for materials.

FRANCINE
Fantastic! Do you have to do an application for the money? I could help out – if you want. I'm a pretty awesome spin merchant. Don't want to stick my nose in where it's not wanted though.

SUZI
No, that would be good! Please come on Saturday morning and we can work on the form.

BARB
Let's begin. Has everyone signed the roll tonight? Suzi? Sorry to be a bore about it everyone, but there's an attendance requirement. I'm sure you all know how it is with Universities and their bureaucracies.
(*Barb returns to the computer to begin her talk. She grabs a pile of papers, and her Powerpoint pointer*)
Okay so as we put on Moodle, Kurt and I will be tag-teaming now for the rest of the semester, as best we can. Sometimes you might get lucky and have us both on the same night.

BARB Tonight's class: Finding the form. *(clicks on powerpoint and slide comes up)*	Week Four Arts-Based Research Methods Finding the form Professor Barb Grattan
BARB (continues) "Why is it", Dewey asks, "that to multitudes, art seems to be an importation into experience from a foreign country and the aesthetic to be a synonym for something artificial?"	John Dewey on Form • Art as an importation into experience from a foreign country • The aesthetic as a synonym for 'artificial'

In his analysis of the aesthetic process, Dewey suggests that in the creation of an artwork, there is **movement from chaos to order**; there is a **quest for form, order, equilibrium, coherence.** He also describes this as **the recovery of union**.	**The aesthetic process**
	• movement from chaos to order;
	• a quest for
	  – form,
	  – order,
	  – equilibrium,
	  – coherence.
	• the recovery of union

There are two factors which should be highlighted from Dewey's analysis. The first is that such processes are potentially aesthetic because of the **heightened experience** offered by the progression to coherence or completion from an initial disruption. Dewey identifies the moment of passage from disturbance into harmony, as the moment of **intensest life**. So let's consider the quest for form.	**Aesthetic potential:** the progression to coherence or completion from an initial disruption. The passage from disturbance into harmony – the moment of **intensest life**.

SUZI
What the hell does that mean?

FRANCINE
Barb, could you just repeat that again? Just the second half of that –?

BARB I think the slide will help clarify, let's see. *(clicks on powerpoint and slide comes up)*	**The Quest for Form** Does form follow function? Or Function form? Does research make a difference?

BARB (continues) *(Barb reads from her notes)* Now let's put two ideas alongside each other – What is said about research: Yes, a quick return to something Kurt raised in the first week of this class *(Barb clicks onto the next slide quickly – somehow it has lost formatting and is unreadable. There is polite attention. Suzi looks around, wondering why no one is pointing out the problem to Barb.)*	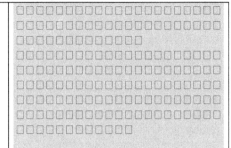
SUZI Barb, your slide is fucked up. *(it resolves and is now readable)* BARB Got it!	The Oxford English Dictionary's definition of research *Systematic investigation into and study of materials and sources, in order to establish facts and reach new conclusions.*
BARB (continues) And what John Dewey, back in the 1920s said about art: It's a dense slide, and that's not ideal I know, oh, and it's very small print I see. It looks like it's lost formatting, damn. Anyway, let me read it to you: *(she reads the whole slide to the class)* So, what do you think? How do these two ideas prompt a consideration of form? Think about it with respect to your own study. Think laterally. *(Beat. Silence.)* Shit. That wasn't like that before class. It doesn't matter, it's the idea that counts: "a systematic investigation into and study of materials". Followed by Dewey: **one must begin with it in the raw** *(Half beat. Barb reads again from the slide.)*	In order to understand the aesthetic in its ultimate and approved forms, **one must begin with it in the raw**; in the events and scenes that hold the attentive eye and ear of man, arousing his interest and affording him enjoyment as he looks and listens: the sights that hold the crowd – the fire-engine rushing by; the machines excavating enormous holes in the earth; the human-fly climbing the steeple-side; the men perched high in air on girders, throwing and catching red-hot bolts. The sources of art in human experience will be learned by him who sees how the tense grace of the ball-player infects the onlooking crowd … the zest of the spectator in poking the wood burning on the hearth and in watching the darting flames and crumbling coals. … The man who poked the sticks of burning wood would say he did it to make the fire burn better; **but he is none the less fascinated by the colourful**

"The sources of art in human experience will be learned by him who sees how the tense grace of the ball-player infects the onlooking crowd … the zest of the spectator in poking the wood burning on the hearth and in watching the darting flames and crumbling coals".	**drama of change enacted before his eyes and imaginatively partakes in it**. (John Dewey, p. 5)
(Beat. Barb has started to appear distracted. She is shuffling her papers. Finds the next page of her lecture.)	
BARB Somewhere between these two paradigms, lies the search for form. This is as relevant and problematic for you in your 'systematic quest' as it was for Dewey. Let's look at how some other philosophers have articulated their quest, and their questions. *(Barb clicks to move to the next slide and the screen goes black.)*	xxxxxxxxx xxxxxxxxx xxxxxxxxx xxxxxxxxx xxxxxxxxx xxxxxxxxx xxxxxxxxx xxxxxxxxx xxxxxxxxx xxxxxxxxx xxxxxxxxx xxxxxxxxx

BARB
Really? You're kidding. I hate these after-hours lectures. Sorry. I don't mean you people – it's just there's not a tech person around after 5. *(Pause).* I have a handout for you, and an activity. I'll be back in a minute.
(Barb leaves and then pops her head back through the door.)
Talk amongst yourselves. About your projects. Do some … collaborative learning.

ANDREA
I was enjoying that. I love John Dewey. We did him in teacher's college, about a million years ago. He's still relevant I reckon. I found one of his articles online the other night. He could have been talking about my kids, my classroom. Sorry, that's probably not relevant. What are we supposed to be doing?

MALCOLM
Collaborative learning.

GERARD
In my experience that's code for an unstructured conversation, frequently unproductive.

FRANCINE
I learn a lot from conversation.

ANDREA
Me too. Gerard and I had a great chat after class last week – don't say we didn't Gerard. You got something out of it, I know. I saw what you posted on Twitter.
Where do you think Barb went? Is something going on?

MALCOLM
Methinks she's having a touch of performance anxiety. Too many weeks in Kurt's shadow, perhaps? Let's make the most of the time. Does anyone have any updates on their projects?

ANDREA
I'm rethinking my question.

FRANCINE
Me too, but in a good way. Not ready to talk about it.

MALCOLM
Well, I've got something to share – I've been thinking all week about the form of my project. And then I started thinking about 'art', the nature and form of art. It was … delicious … I'd spent all day in meetings – policy, stakeholder accountability, benchmarking, quality assurance. And then I got all my notes and images and ideas together for my project and I said to them, no, this is true, I said, how do I honour you? I think I was just about to get a reply when my wife walked in –
'who are you talking to?' she says?

'my mate Cziksentmihalyi' I say.

She says, 'ask him if he wants to come to dinner, there's plenty'.

So, I asked him, and he said 'yes', I mean 'da, spasibo' (he's very polite)

That's not the best of it though. After dinner, I googled 'art and poets' – not the most rigorous approach to research I know, don't tell Barb, or Kurt for that matter.

Anyway, I found this poem by Rudyard Kipling. Hit the nail on the head – for me, just for where I'm at right now. I've got it here somewhere. Talk amongst yourselves … as Barb would say.

(he starts going through files on his ipad)

FRANCINE

What's that Suzi? *(Francine tries to look in the top of Suzi's overstuffed bag)*

SUZI

It's nothing.

FRANCINE

No it's not. Could I have a look? Please? Is that your sewing – you were telling me about those flowers the other day.

SUZI

It was just an idea I had, for my project.

FRANCINE

Come on, please. I'm interested. We're all interested, aren't we?

SUZI

It's something I've been working on. I want to start a craft group in my building, so I thought I'd make something that was inspired by … it sounds ridiculous, but inspired by coming to this class – it started out as a pillow case. But now, I see it as um more than that, like it says something about *me*. I'm still working on it. This blue is for the flowers in the beds next to the playground, they remind me of some flowers we have back in South Sudan. They've just started blooming …

(Barb returns while Suzi is talking, with a pile of handouts. She listens and then quietly passes the handouts to Andrea to distribute. She looks at everyone, almost speaks, then disappears again.)

MALCOLM
I found it. The poem. Do you want to hear a bit of it?
(Malcolm parodies a declamatory style of performance in his delivery)
They built a tower to shiver the sky and wrench the stars apart,
Till the Devil grunted behind the bricks "It's striking, but is it Art?"
The stone was dropped at the quarry-side and the idle derrick swung,
While each man talked of the aims of Art, and each in an alien tongue.

They fought and they talked in the North and the South, they talked and they fought in the West,
Till the waters rose on the pitiful land, and the poor Red Clay had rest –
Had rest til the dank, blank-canvas dawn when the dove was preened to start,
And the Devil bubbled below the keel: "It's human, but is it Art?"

There's more, but you get the gist …
(There is polite, if somewhat uncomprehending, applause. Malcolm bows, in an exaggerated style, then staggers slightly but covers it up, and sits down quietly)

SUZI
I don't get it. Sorry Malcolm but –

GERARD
Actually, I have something to share too. It appears that the data projector isn't working, so I'll have to show you on my computer.

(the class gathers around as Gerard reveals his 'work of art' – there is a pause while they attempt to work out what they are looking at.)

FRANCINE
Are we looking at a graph?

GERARD
Yes.

FRANCINE
Would there be a point to this Gerard? How is this arts-based research?

GERARD
Can't you see it? Here, Malcolm, you're a man of science. Come closer and take a look at this table.

MALCOLM
It looks to me like a graphic representation of a survey of some kind.

GERARD
It is. It's my first cut of the data – well not really data. It was a pilot study I did last year with principals in my region, but I thought it would be instructive to analyse this survey I did. And here it is. You don't see it, do you? It's a perfect bell curve. Look at the symmetry. Their engagement with professional learning is directly proportional to the number of years they've been in the job – it's amazing.

(Barb finally returns to the room. She's carrying an old fashioned cassette tape recorder and a cheap, beaten up, yellowing notebook. The class notice her return and resume their seats.)

BARB
The tale is as old as the Eden Tree – and new as the new-cut tooth –
For each man knows ere his lip-thatch grows he is master of Art and Truth;

83

And each man hears as the twilight nears, to the beat of his dying heart,
The Devil drum on the darkened pane: "You did it, but was it Art?"
Rudyard Kipling, 1890.

I'm sorry about tonight everyone. For some inexplicable reason, I sort of … lost the plot. I don't believe in making excuses to students, but I just have to say this has never happened to me before, in 25 years of lecturing. Maybe that's the point. I made an error of judgement, coming in tonight with my lecture on Finding the Form, all prepared. I wanted to give you some substance, some gristle, to trouble away at while each of you finds your way through your project. And, as I prepared, I became immersed in the theory – theorising about an artist, or a researcher, finding the form to hold their work. It's something I've grappled with many times, not as an artist, not like Kurt or you Andrea, in your work with your children, or you too Suzi, but as a researcher, trying to make sense out of life's experiences, systematically.
Anyway, as soon as I walked back into this room, Umberto Eco in one hand, Suzanne Langer in the other, I simply, couldn't find the words – they seemed inadequate to the task. You're already doing it – finding form for your inquiry, through your inquiry. I'm not actually sure there's much I can teach you about this approach to research, right at this moment. And that statement's a first for me, in 25 years as well.

What I think I might be able to do, though, is share something that I was reminded of recently, when you were all presenting your proposals for your projects. I remembered a moment when art, life and research connected for me. It was a long time ago.

FRANCINE
Hence the cassette player.

BARB
Hence the cassette player – I'm surprised you knew what it was. These are recordings from a Ceiledh on the Western Highlands of

Scotland, some 20 odd years ago. Oh sorry, a ceiledh is like a folk concert – traditional music, dance, poems, a celebration of the ancient and the immediate, the mythical and the everyday. I was interested in … No, let me just play this for you so you can hear for yourself and maybe you can answer the devil – "It's human, but is it Art?"

(Scottish traditional music begins to play – an immediate hush falls over them, they are all stopped in their tracks and quite moved. Slowly, scene ends.)

INTERMEZZO 3: ONE WAY OR ANOTHER

(The previous class has concluded, and all the students have left. Barb is packing up her notes, computer, tape recorder etc. Kurt appears in the doorway. He's holding an email in his hand.)

KURT
Hi.

BARB
(surprised) Hi.

KURT
How did it go?

BARB
Checking up on me?

KURT
Of course not. I was working late, in my office, just thought I'd see how things went.

BARB
Well, they missed you. How did it go, you ask? Hmm. Where to begin. It was shit and it was great. I wouldn't mind leaving it at that. I think perhaps I underprepared. Next time will be easier.

KURT
That's great. Glad to hear it. I hope they didn't give you a hard time.

BARB
Why would they? Actually, quite the opposite, they were remarkably sanguine – given my … performance. And they're a great bunch – becoming very self-directed, all of them, in one way or another.

KURT

Well you know. Students can sometimes. They can take advantage of your good nature. You know, cross the line. Sometimes, they can rip your heart out and eat it, if you give them half a chance.

BARB

Yes I've noticed that as well in my 30 years of this work.

(Kurt shakes his head in frustration and turns to leave)

BARB

Is there something going on? Is it Francine? She's got a bit of a crush you know.

KURT

Not her too. God, these women. **You** know I'm gay, right?

BARB

You know if there's a problem with a student there are protocols, Kurt. The University has to protect the welfare of the student.

KURT

Protocols. What about me? What about my welfare? I should have known better than to try to talk to you Barb. When it comes to the crunch, you're always going to take their side.

BARB

Whose side? The student's? The University's? What's going on? Are you in some kind of trouble? If there was a disciplinary matter I would have heard about it. You really need to tell me what's going on.

KURT

Why, so you can call in the thought police? Have me shown off the premises. You'd like that wouldn't you.

BARB
No, actually I wouldn't.

KURT
Wouldn't you? Really?

BARB
I might be a pain in the ass bureaucrat to you, but I'm not completely blind. I see your talent, your intellectual talent I mean. And you have more charisma than one mortal is entitled to, especially in our line of work, you little shit.

KURT
Sorry Barb. It's not you. Really. I'm just so fucking overwhelmed. I've gotta go. Talk to you later –
(he leaves)

BARB
(calls after him) Call me. No, I'll call you. Kurt? Shit!

(end of scene)

SCENE / CLASS 5: TELLING STORIES
(WHOSE STORIES?)

(SUZI and FRANCINE are sitting in a Common Room on the ground floor of the Fitzroy Flats where Suzi lives. The room is set up with 10 tables pushed together in the middle, and about 20 chairs. There are arts supplies on the table, and some sewing materials as well. They each have a cup of tea and are talking. The room is bright and cheerful.)

SUZI

I don't know why nobody is here. They said they come. The two ladies that live either side of me on the 6th floor, they said they was coming. Maybe the kids are sick. I'm sorry you came here for no reason.

FRANCINE

Don't be! I'm really glad I came and get to see where you live. It's a really cool place. I know you said you liked your last apartment better, but this is amazing. You have 3 huge bedrooms, the whole apartment is so big, and secure, and warm in the winter, cool in the summer – you don't have to pay for those utilities, which is really expensive, seriously –

SUZI

I know, but it's druggies here. Like *(motions toward the outside)* I just have to keep my eye on Buster out there all the time. Rishana is with her father but when she gets old enough to want to go outside with Buster, I'm going to be very scared. There's bad people around here. They go in the lifts with cigarettes, they stare at you, sometimes they say stuff. It's not that nice. Drugs.

FRANCINE

But that's why it's so cool you're starting this group. Should we talk about it?

SUZI

Okay. Let me check on Buster.

(she walks to the door and calls out)

Hey! Buster! Buster, come here!

(nothing)

Boy you better get over here or I'm coming out there and it's not gonna be pretty.

(nothing)

FRANCINE

Do you want me to go out and –

SUZI

HEY!!!

(he acknowledges her)

Don't stray from that playground ok? If you want to go somewhere you got to come in here and ask me. Alright? *(beat)* Alright??? Say alright.

(beat. He says it, offstage, and she is satisfied. She comes back to the table)

Alright. Let's talk about it.

FRANCINE

So I was thinking, you are like in totally the best position of all of us to do the kind of research project that Kurt was talking about the other day as 'embodied research for social change'. To represent your kind of truth.

SUZI

What's the truth?, that's the question. Like you said in class.

FRANCINCE

Totally. That's why I believe in this stuff, because I don't believe there is only one version. Like what is it you rely on? Evidence, other people's opinions, or your own gut instinct? Not everyone relies on numbers, and I'm sick of people using only numbers to make decisions about my life. It just isn't good enough.

SUZI

I think the truth is hard to figure out sometimes. Like with this asshole Abraham that is the father of my kids. He left me completely alone when I had Buster. Completely. Like his family spit on me when they saw me in the street in Footscray, because he said I was lying that he was the father. So I got kicked out of home, I ended up in tough times, really bad times. But I had Buster, I got on with it, I set up a house and everything. No one to help me, just me myself and I. And then all of a sudden when Buster was like 3, Abraham come back and say he want to see his son, he wants to rename him, all this shit.

FRANCINE

Oh my god, what?

SUZI

Exactly. So I had to go to court, he got DNA tested, all the rest of it. Then he starts spending time with his son, because in Sudanese culture you just can't deny the father if he wants to see his children. He actually stole all Buster's pictures off my facebook and put them on his facebook like "this is my son" all shit, like so proud. I was so pissed! Anyway. Somehow I ended up getting pregnant again after that.

FRANCINE

Oh Suzi, that's terrible! *(they are laughing)*

SUZI

I didn't mind. I wanted a second one. I dated this other guy in the meantime, a Sudanese guy from Sydney who was really good to me and to Buster, but you know in the end he didn't want to marry me because I was already – you know, like not a virgin. So his family wouldn't accept it. So when Abraham started coming around again I just figured oh well.

FRANCINE

Do you want to be with him?

SUZI

I do and I don't. I mean, he's always been a player. I hate it. He thinks he's so hot and all the girls want him, but it's just so frustrating. To the point where after I had Rishana he actually came to the hospital with another girlfriend! It was ridiculous. He had been in the delivery WITH me – pretty unusual for a Sudanese dude – and he even cut the cord. So I was really happy, thought we had our family, but then he did that when Rishana was like 3 days old and I'm lying in there with a hospital gown on looking all nasty. That was bad.

FRANCINE

What a jerk. Jesus.

SUZI

He is and he isn't. And now that I have 2 kids with him, I figure he is gonna have to deal with me. But on the other hand, I feel like if I keep going with him, I will just never know what is the truth, and what just looks like the truth – like what Kurt was talking about in class that time.

FRANCINE

Yeah, good point. But you know, I don't know if any of us ever really know what the truth is. Like does it even exist? I think it's just everyone's got their own versions. And you hope to god that you find someone else who has a similar sense of the truth.

SUZI

Yeah but it's got to be more than that right? You are talking about values there. And the research truth is a different kinda thing altogether. I mean, seriously. You got to be able to say something is the truth, so and so, or what's the point? Seriously.

FRANCINE

Well I don't know. What is the point? Is there still a point, even if the focus of your project isn't 'truth' or making things better? That's what I was trying to say, it's got to be worth something.

SUZI
(laughing)
See this is the kind of shit that drives Gerard crazy!!!

(they laugh)

FRANCINE
I know, I thought he was going to blow a gasket last week!

SUZI
What's a gasket?

FRANCINE
Just a figure of speech. But seriously, let's talk about that in terms of both our projects. For you, you want to run a group here that does drawing and painting, right? That then you make into sewing items.

SUZI
That's it. Like I want it to be sewing because that's a very Sudanese thing, a woman thing, and something I myself would like to learn. But we got to start with drawing or painting the pictures, the designs, and then we can transfer them onto the cloth. Make pillows or whatever. Or those things on the couch.

FRANCINE
Like you have upstairs?

SUZI
Yeah –

FRANCINE
Those are doilies, we call them doilies.

SUZI
Yeah that's what every Sudanese has. We can make them, and clothes for the kids if we get really good. I'm just really disappointed these girls didn't come today – I thought they would come. They're

nice, but it's just hard to find a reason to get together and talk, because I think we could be friends, you know? But we really only see each other in the hallway, or the lift. We don't have any reason to like knock on each other's doors is all. And another thing: if we had a chance to get to know them, then we could be friends but our kids could be friends too, even better.

FRANCINE
Good point.

SUZI
Because it's important to meet your neighbours, make community. It's safer too. You know, it was so different in Egypt how everyone spoke to each other, looked after each other's children, even though there was a lot of racism too. But it's different here.

FRANCINE
Like a white thing you mean? Like the isolation of white culture?

SUZI
No, it's not a white thing, just a western cultural thing. Everyone's too busy and likes to stay private even if that makes them sad and lonely! It's weird, I'm telling you. And Sudanese are slipping into that lifestyle too fast, and it's sad. Like take me: I'm so isolated now. When Abraham doesn't come over, or now I know you, but still – then I just have to stay here with the baby, and Buster gets so bored and acts up, it's not good. It's depressing for all of us. Even though I am glad I've got the apartment and all.

FRANCINE
Is that what made you think about the arts group for your project? It's so perfect for this place – I mean, you can get class credit, but also there must be dozens of mothers in these 5 buildings that would benefit from that. The talking, the collaboration –

SUZI

Yeah and also we can make things to hang in our apartments! It would be really good. If anyone comes.

FRANCINE

They'll come. It might just take a while to get the word around. What gave you the idea for it?

SUZI

Well a couple years back when I first left school I went to this place for single mums, called River Nile Learning Centre, and we did a visual arts exhibition at a place out in Footscray which was so cool. We made screen prints, we talked about politics and racism, and fashion – stuff like that – and then we made art about it. And we put it up in that place, and all these people came to see it at the opening, I loved that! And we did a performance too. Speaking of which – I thought we'd have like 20 people today.

FRANCINE

It's alright. We can pass out more fliers for next time.

SUZI

Anyway, it was a really good thing. We just got to know each other so much while we were doing that, and there were lots of different people there – Somali, Ethiopians, everything – and we had a great time just talking, eating together. Like that.

FRANCINE

Well I think that's where the truth is. Not so much in the making stuff but in what happens while you're making it.

SUZI

Exactly.

FRANCINE

And so do you think it matters if its art that brings you together, or anything else?

SUZI

Yeah I do. I think art is different because it always brings out the personal – like it makes you talk about yourself, to fill in that artwork. It's very personal if you know what I mean. If we did something else, like bingo or – I don't know – it wouldn't work like that. Even sport. That can be good to bring people together, but not necessarily to talk about yourself the way you can in arts stuff. I love the arts. I wanted to be an actress on TV actually.

FRANCINE

Me too! What did you want to be on?

SUZI

'Neighbours'. They had auditions. And I thought for some reason they're gonna put a Black girl on there over another pasty white person, but they didn't. I was pretty stupid to think that, but you know there's so many non-white people in this country but no one admits it. You'd never know from watching tv. It pissed me off.

FRANCINE

Did you audition?

SUZI

Yeah I did actually. But Buster was like 1 year old then, and everything was too hard. Plus racism, you can't forget that.

FRANCINE

Well this is what Kurt was talking about. To change that, you have got to do projects like yours, ones that build community for social change, as well as, what was it that Kurt said, letting you make arts that others can see so they can understand more about you and your culture or your own experience – which in a way also creates social change if you think about it.

SUZI

Social change would be good.

FRANCINE
Totally!

SUZI
You see Buster out there?

(Francine gets up and looks out the window)

FRANCINE
Yeah, he's fine.

SUZI
So what are you going to do?

FRANCINE
Well it's kinda weird. There's this famous Australian lady called Dorothy Hewett, who was a playwright and activist and generally interesting woman. She died in 2002.

SUZI
What does she have to do with anything?

FRANCINE
Well this is for my Honours thesis. I'm calling it *The Empty Room: The unreconstructed later life of Dorothy Hewett.* Isn't that cool?

SUZI
What's an Honours thesis? And what is that word –?

FRANCINE
Unreconstructed? Like, not fixed up. The honours is like an extra year on top of an undergrad degree. It's a project-based extra kind of qualification, and then sets you up to do a Masters degree or a PhD if you want to.

SUZI
Whoa, you must be smart.

FRANCINE

No, I'm just – I don't know what I'm doing. My parents are both lawyers and –

SUZI

Oh shit! Here I was feeling like we kind of understood each other.

FRANCINE

We do! Don't say that, it makes me feel terrible! We DO understand each other, I hate law and I hate that they're pressuring me to 'do something' with my life.

SUZI

I would love someone to pressure me about doing something with my life! Every time I try to do something with my life everyone tells me I'm being stupid and I should just focus on looking after my kids.

FRANCINE

Well I guess both ways are hard. I'm sorry you don't have that support, that sucks.

SUZI

No it's cool. So what are you doing actually? Like, what is it?

FRANCINE

I'm not sure yet but I think I'm going to devise a play. A performed prose poem (triple P), inspired by Dorothy because she wrote these crazy plays that were mostly poetry and which were pretty much impossible to stage.

SUZI

What do you mean?

FRANCINE

Like the theatres could never put them on because they were too hard, too expensive, too confusing. But everyone still loved her because she was full of passion, she had a great love of literature and writing, and she was so fierce. She was such a champion of women.

SUZI
Was she gay or something?

FRANCINE
No she wasn't actually. She had like 3 husbands and 5 or 6 kids and she kicked ass. I just like her because she was one of those really important 20th century Australian playwrights that got written out of history, and because I want to be like her.

SUZI
You want to have 3 husbands? You can have mine to start with.

(they laugh)

FRANCINE
So yeah, basically I'm going to try to make a performance. I think I'm going to use the arts-based method called performance ethnography, but I've got to still figure out the ethnography bit.

SUZI
Well if you need an actress let me know. I was almost on Neighbours you know!

FRANCINE
Awesome, I will! Maybe we can perform it together, wouldn't that be cool!?

SUZI
Well I don't want to make you look bad, but if you're up for it –!

FRANCINE
Oh yeah, whatever! I think I can give you a run for your money!

SUZI
Just give me your money, don't worry about the run –

FRANCINE
Hey maybe we can keep helping each other as we put these projects together.

SUZI
That could be cool.

FRANCINE
I'd really love that.

SUZI
You can put pressure on me for my future.

(they both smile)

FRANCINE
Yeah sure.
(beat)
Hey, I don't think anybody's coming. Should we go back up to your place and make some lunch?

SUZI
Good idea. Let's bounce.

(They each grab a box of arts & sewing supplies, and head out. When Suzi opens the door, she looks to the playground):

Buster! Move your ass!

(end of scene)

SCENE / CLASS 6: QUESTIONS OF REPRESENTATION

(Andrea and Gerard are sitting at a café with glasses of wine in front of each of them.)

GERARD
So what are you doing and how can I help you?

ANDREA
Well *(laughs out of embarrassment or annoyance at his arrogance)* – well thanks, but I'm not sure I – you know this was Kurt's idea, don't you? Buddying each of us up – I think he thought we should go together because we're both education. But I'm doing ok on my own you know. I'm working through my process, step by step. And I'm finding the journaling really helpful.

GERARD
Why don't you just tell me a bit more about your project and then we can go from there?

ANDREA
Sure. I'll tell you mine if you tell me yours – we can help each other. *(she gathers herself. She refuses to get angry)*
So. This unit is part of my Masters in Education. I'm always looking for a way to capture something 'essential' about the learning that's happening with my Grade 3s. You know the learning they're doing through the arts. And with this project, I really want to use the arts to express the research as well, if that makes sense. And I'm really committed to finding something that I can take back to my school, something that can assist me to change the culture of my school through my research –

GERARD
Honourable. What's wrong with your current school culture? That's my area you know, educational leadership.

ANDREA

I would say the problems at my school have nothing to do with leadership actually –

GERARD

Well, like it or not, everything has to do with leadership. School cultures are established and maintained from the top down, as neoliberal as that sounds.

ANDREA

It actually sounds pretty depressing. Right, so why don't you tell me about your project? It sounds like you are pretty certain about what you're doing.

GERARD

No, no – please finish. I think you were saying –

(beat)

ANDREA

Well, I've recently taken on this arts teacher role across the early years. I told you about the art project with the Grade 3s in my first presentation – if you recall. And, I've been working with Shakespeare in the year 1-2 classroom. First I was going to do something with the Grade 3s and their visual arts project, but now I'm thinking that I could use the Shakespeare project as a multidisciplinary approach to peer learning and ZPD – I'd like to do something with that.

(beat)

GERARD

Interesting. So you're hoping to change your school culture to an Elizabethan one?

(she doesn't laugh)

GERARD

Just kidding. Well that's very, um … that's great. A good match for this arts-based research class really isn't it? You must be feeling very, uh – well, confident for one thing.

ANDREA

No I'm not feeling confident at all. It might fit well here with this unit, and with Kurt and Barb, but it's a terrible fit for my school, mainly because my principal is a lot like you.

GERARD

That can't be a bad thing.

ANDREA

That's not a put-down –

GERARD

I'd have to disagree with –

ANDREA

Well if you'd stop interrupting me I'll explain what I meant.

(his anger flares at this confrontation, but he holds his tongue.)

GERARD

Feel free.

ANDREA

I think I … I really think that – *(deep breath)* – I got into teaching originally because I loved kids and I believed that good pedagogical experiences in the first 10 years is a radical act that can change their lives dramatically. No pun intended. Drastically. And I wanted to change society, so I guess you'd say I came to both teaching and the arts from a social change perspective. I believe that the way that students and student learning is represented is powerful – either as a vehicle for liberation or oppression. I loved all that Paulo Freire stuff we read in my teaching degree. Remember? So I believe every child has the right to learn in his or her own way, and to not be tested by someone else's standards. Obviously I'm at odds with the current standardised testing imperatives sweeping our sector, but that's another conversation for later. Or never. I guess what I'm saying is, I believe in using arts approaches in education because in my experience it offers the best chance, the most egalitarian chance, to all students to find their form, to find how they can express their identity and encounter learning in their own way. That's it.

GERARD
Um … well, that's very noble, but what are you actually going to do?

ANDREA
Gerard, can you – do you think you could lighten up just a little? Like, ease up a bit? This stuff is personal. Arts-based research is close to the bone. And to be honest, it's not very encouraging when you, I don't know, well, when you come across so judgemental all the time. Could you get down off your high horse for a minute so we can have a conversation? You might have been my boss, but in this class, we're equals.

GERARD
I'm not judging you. Believe it or not, I find your perspective really quite instructive. I probably have more to learn from you – or least something to learn – than you do from me. Bet you didn't think you'd hear me saying that.

ANDREA
You've been coming into class with a great big chip on your shoulder and it's a little off-putting to be honest. I know you don't mean to be, but its kind of aggressive. And while I've taken to this kind of research more quickly than you –

GERARD
Hold on, now, that's unfair.

ANDREA

– while I might be showing more aptitude for ABR, you're wasting precious time shutting people down and criticising all the time. You don't seem to be open to learning anything new or to really sharing or risking anything much – except that perfect bell curve the other night. It makes it really hard for the rest of us. It's not respectful.

GERARD

Well I'm sorry!

ANDREA

Thank you.

(beat. Dead silence. Both embarrassed)

GERARD

I guess I'm feeling a bit, I don't know. Disappointed about all of this. I was ready to go with my quantitative study, had nearly finished the ethics application even. I'm a very efficient person. I'm very driven. That's who I am – that's my research identity. And quant research is how I want my intellectual property to be represented – that's my 'truth'.

To be perfectly honest, I'm not doing this for 'an experience' like some in the class, I'm doing it for an end goal and that end goal is very career-oriented. And I just don't feel like there is any room in there for me. For my kind of perspective. I don't feel respected. So it's kind of funny that you accuse me of –

ANDREA

Well I can understand that. But – can't you make it work to your advantage somehow?

GERARD

I just feel like a fish out of water. I don't have anything in common with anyone else, even Malcolm, the medical scientist – he's the worst of the lot of you. Sorry, that was rude. Let's get back to our 'collaborative brainstorm' session. I'm not really sure how I can help you think through your project Andrea.

ANDREA
I think I do. You know how I said you're like my principal? Now don't get angry again! –

GERARD
Yeah, no, that's fine –

ANDREA
Well I was thinking that maybe it's good for me to talk it through with someone like him. So that I can get inside his head a bit more, and figure out a way to do this project that makes sense to him.

GERARD
Okay.

ANDREA
Well, as I said, I've only recently become the arts teacher at my school. For the past seven years I've taught the Prep-to-1s, but I needed a break. Everyone does, believe me. So I feel kind of insecure about teaching the arts, but I've found that I like it. So I thought maybe the kids would feel like that too. My own kids – I've got 2 – my own kids Dana and Riley are pretty sporty, not really the arty types. So I want to pitch to the kids in my school like that – the ones who don't see the value, aren't naturally drawn to it, or think they have to be good to do it.

GERARD
Okay, that all makes sense. Do you have permission to do a research project in your own school, if your principal is hostile?

ANDREA
He's not hostile, I didn't mean that. In fact, he's only been there a year and a half and he's been strangely supportive of me. I think he recognises a need to change the school culture, and doesn't exactly

know how. So he's got behind me, encouraged the Masters, and even this research project, in principle, but he has the mind of a mathematics person, of a businessman, and I'm afraid when I pitch my project to him he will get scared and shut it down.

GERARD
Okay, well then I can say this. Lead with numbers. Lead with measureables, and outcomes, and benefit to the school, don't lead with airy fairy notions of social justice and inclusion and brightening up the school – that is not where his anxiety lives. It's in proving that he is competent to facilitate a rise in the academic outcomes, enrolments, and community links of his school. So if you can help him do that, he will let you do whatever you want, guaranteed.

ANDREA
That's creepy.

GERARD
What is?

ANDREA
I've been trying to figure out how his mind works for months now. And you just summed it up in like 2 sentences.

GERARD
You just needed to talk to someone who thinks like him.

ANDREA
You know what's funny? My husband is exactly like him – in a different business. He's an engineer who recently got laid off from the Ford factory in Geelong, so things have been kind of – you know.

GERARD
I'm sorry to hear that.

ANDREA
No what I mean is, his mind works exactly that way, so I never talk about this stuff at home.

GERARD
Why not?

ANDREA
I don't know. It's not him, it's me. He's always been the brains in our family, and I –

GERARD
No offense, but I don't think you doing an arts-based masters is going to change that!

ANDREA
Gerard –

GERARD
Well I'm sorry if –

ANDREA
No, what I'm saying is, I guess, I don't want to come home talking about being excited about my work when he's just been retrenched. That's just adding insult to injury.

GERARD
Maybe. Or maybe it will remind him that he still has something to share, and that you still need him even though he isn't the main breadwinner right now.

(Beat. Andrea starts to say something, then stops. She gets teary. Gerard gets embarrassed).

GERARD
Well anyway, nothing's perfect. I'm happy to talk more later about the specifics of how to represent your project to him, if you want. Totally up to you.

ANDREA
Thanks. Now it's your turn.

GERARD
Well, I'm doing a Doctorate of Education in Educational Leadership looking at school renewal and parent involvement, which is quite a coincidence in light of what you were saying about your own school. That's actually my area of focus – how to change school cultures – but I'm looking more at working with families, ie. parents to do so. It's a gap in the literature.

ANDREA
It's a certain kind of parent isn't it?

GERARD
Well the principles of parent engagement are universal, not only middle class or professional parents.

ANDREA
Yeah but principles aren't practices are they?

GERARD
Ideally, yes. Yes they are.

ANDREA
'Ideally' has a very tenuous hold on reality. Kind of like the verisimilitude they were talking about in class a couple of weeks ago?

GERARD
Well it's my job to make it real. Not just appear as real but remain false.

ANDREA
Well good luck with that.

GERARD
Thank you. But what I don't know is how to do something in here that is arts-based that would contribute to that study. I'd rather it contribute even though it's completely off the map of my proposed quantitative study of 150 Victorian schools. You can't use arts-based methods for that.

ANDREA
Okay let's think about that. Can't you? If you can get parents or teachers – who are you measuring?

GERARD
It's principals, teachers and parents.

ANDREA
Okay if you're getting them all to do surveys, why can't you use some open-ended questions that can only be answered using arts-based responses? Is it possible?

GERARD
Anything's possible, but my study doesn't have anything at all to do with ABR, so it wouldn't make any sense.

ANDREA
Maybe you're not thinking broadly enough. You don't have to have them all paint pictures for god's sake. I think this might be a really great way to explore the question of representation that Kurt was talking about a while back. What if you, say, used narrative – like get the parents to 'tell you a story' of their best engagement with the school, for example ...? So we see the school through the eyes of the parents – that's the lens. By doing that you're framing the research findings in a way that speaks directly to those people who are most affected by them. You should have a look at the Curious Schools

website (www.utas.edu.au/education/curious-schools) – might give you some inspiration.

GERARD
Okay, say more –

ANDREA
I don't know, or – my understanding of ABR is like you could do a kind of mixed method thing where you still have your hot-shit quantitative statistical analysis of the schools' numbers on parent engagement (if such a thing exists), but also include like one or two sets of parents from each school to share being the researcher with you. To be co-researchers.

GERARD
But how would they do that without knowing anything about research?

ANDREA
Yeah but YOU know about research. That's what you bring. And THEY know about their school, and themselves, their kid, and their family. They know what they want, what they're not getting, and they might have good insights about how to get it. Insights that you yourself would never think of.

GERARD
I don't know –

ANDREA
Like for instance, what if you gave 10 of them a flip cam to make a video diary about their school engagement? It could be totally up to them what they film. It could be them filming their kid talking about the school and how they have no PTA, or it could be them interviewing their partner about how the school always puts parent teacher night on when you can't make it home in time, or – I don't know –

GERARD
What if they did something like the parent interviews the principal? To kind of turn the power thing around? Just for an hour, I mean –

ANDREA
Yes! That would be sooo interesting! I think you're on to something. And what about the teachers? What if you asked the teachers to write a story about their perfect school-parent relationship or event, starting with "Once upon a time ..." –

GERARD
Okay, that's a bit too far for me –

(they laugh)

ANDREA
Yeah right. Well, I do think you're on to something Gerard. Arts-based research is always evolving. This article I was reading last night says something about it being so many different things, including different theoretical frames like poststructuralist, post-paradigmatic (whatever that is) –

GERARD
I don't know, I'll give it some thought. But I'm not about to ask them all to start doing an interpretive dance to show me how they think parents and schools should work together.

ANDREA
No, I don't think anyone wants that. I should be getting home, Ron will be wondering where I am.

GERARD
Sure. Thanks Andrea. I think you're right – you really do have a handle on this arts-based research caper.

ANDREA
Who knew? Something at Uni I'm good at! See you later.

(end of scene)

INTERMEZZO 4 – ART AS TRUTH? HOLDING ON TO THE MUSE

(Kurt sits in his office, Miles Davis playing quietly in the background. He talks into a tape recorder – is this research? Diary? We are not sure.)

KURT
I feel like I've lost my best friend.
Music, for me, used to be the place where I went to remember who I am. But now it feels like an ex-boyfriend who is just smirking at me, reminding me of who I used to be. Of course, I know identity's not that simple. I can't smirk at myself, my sax certainly doesn't snigger my way. But Christ, it's like I've lost something that I can't get back.

I feel like a smack addict who keeps explaining away his slips. First I started teaching high school, and I thought that was the end, I really did. I prayed that none of my music mates found out. I refused to put anything about it on Facebook, and wouldn't friend any teaching colleagues. And I found that I love teaching, I really do! But I just couldn't believe I was doing it. Like a whole identity shift thing. Like a personality shift, a midlife crisis – at 29! Okay, Saturn return. Yep, got it.

I thought of getting the scholarship to do the PhD like a great big community arts grant. Four years of funding to just do music, and then write about it! How cool. I knew it was too good to be true. As mum used to say, 'No lunch is free' or 'if it seems too good to be true, it probably is!'. She was right. It was kind of a deal with the devil which on my good days still feels like I'm getting paid a lot of money to make art, and on my bad days feels like I've sold out and don't know who I am anymore. Life is compromise I guess, but I almost can't stand to be on FaceBook any more, congratulating all my friends who are now making it big. They don't get quite as excited about my academic promotions let's just say, as they do about winning their Grammy or Oscar for soundtracks. But I'm

117

trying to be grateful for what I've got, which – even I realise – is considerable.

I think it really comes back to my arrogance or you might say self confidence, which was drummed into us in music school – it is absolutely totally necessary to stay alive as a musician – and also comes in handy in this business. I guess I was just so naïve, I just thought I could do it my way and would never be co-opted like these mole rats you see everywhere in their cubicles, you know? Academics? But then one thing led to another – too many carrots! I was flattered probably, and – to be fair, it was fun in the beginning. God I sound like I'm doing a 12 step testimonial here.

When they offered me the job, I was like 'alright I'll do it, but I'm only doing music, I'm not getting caught up in the fucking airless cycle of paper-writing, conferencing and clawing my way up the greasy pole'. It's disgusting. It's like humanity at its worst. And yet – here I am. I walk around feeling patronised by the poststructuralists and 'pure theory' assholes in this department. Like why do I even care? How did I end up caring? Totally fucking ridiculous. Is it just my competitive streak? I'm seriously confused.

And when students go for those types over me, I'm cut. I am! It's ridiculous. I feel like I'm walking around like a ball of pulsing nerves, just waiting to be bruised. With the academics, I feel relentlessly insecure and don't feel like I fit in. With the students I feel jealous of everyone they like more or think is smarter. With my fellow music researchers I feel like an imposter now, an in-betweener. And yet my arrogance still rises up in equal measure, telling me I'm one of the few amongst us who has actually been trained, who has worked professionally, who doesn't need this gig like 'they' do. But every day, I need it a little more. Every day, it creeps further into my soul and the more cavalier about it I try to be, the worse it gets.

Students like Jaime really get under my skin. She's so fucking sure she knows more than me, more than everyone else. How did I end up with someone like her in the beginning? When I was doing my PhD I really didn't bother my supervisors at all! I respected them, I think, and figured it was up to me to just get on with it. But these students – it's like they own you. And another thing – they don't even come in with any ideas, they want you to do it all for them. I mean, what are you DOING here??? I wish I could just supervise jazz students, and say no to everything else but it doesn't work that way.

I'd really like to tell Jaime she's a naïve dipshit and she should just withdraw or find another supervisor. But I can't do that. I wish I could swap her for someone like Ajak. I mean, she'd make a brilliant researcher, but no one realises it – least of all her. She has so much talent and so much understanding of this work, and also the most important part – a healthy scepticism of this western knowledge paradigm. I would love to work more with her, but that's what happens – students like Ajak end up without childcare, or overwhelmed by the racism of the academy, and they leave. And the Jaime's rise and rise. It's like she hates my guts and has a crush on me at the same time – I know Jaime thinks I'm not gay. Why does she even feel she has the right to make such insinuations? Would a male student ever try and seduce his lesbian supervisor and be like 'I know you think you're gay but you're not? You just need to be with a man!" I mean, that would be harassment. Maybe she is harassing me, I don't know anymore. I feel so uncomfortable so much of the time, I can't tell what's appropriate or inappropriate to be honest.

I try to stay under the radar, like Tom suggested, as much as I can. But it's not my personality, and I keep popping up – I don't even know how it happens, I swear to fucking god. I'm probably in the wrong business. But I keep going up and down on this roller coaster. I think the worst part of this transitional period for me is that I feel almost constantly like I don't know where I belong. I have thought of myself as an artist, a musician for so long, that to think of myself as an academic is like the witness relocation program. I just … I want to lose myself in this new life, I do. I'm passionate about it, sometimes. And I think I can bring freshness to it, in some undefinable way. But when I lift my head up and look around, I feel lonely and like my sprinter's energy is rapidly evaporating. I don't want to end up like Barb, jaded and numb most of the time. Or any of them to be honest. I don't know if I've actually met an academic yet who I thought 'wow, I really want to be like him'. That's pretty sad, and how is that viable, if I have no role models? Even the ones interested in social justice so often act like colonising assholes in private. It's all just so disillusioning.

I was interviewing a principal the other day for this research project and he said "the hardest thing about artists becoming teachers is them learning how to put themselves aside. Making it about the students, not them". And I think – as much as I REALLY hated him saying that – I think he's right, and maybe for researchers too. I can see it in my students, and in myself too. Not consciously of course, but unconsciously. Maybe that's why I'm always trying to do arts-based research, and to propose classroom work as 'collaboration' rather than teaching and learning. I thought it was because I was egalitarian, socially inclusive, rebellious, the arts-based engagement guru. But maybe it's just because I have such a big goddamned ego that I can't stand to write myself out of the picture.

(beat. His email 'pings' and he switches off the tape recorder.)

(end of scene)

SCENE 7: RESEARCHER AS ARTIST / ARTIST AS RESEARCHER

(Kurt's email alert pings, pings and pings again – 3 in a row. He slams his desk, his shoulders fall, he hangs his head. When he finally looks up, he turns off the music and reads the first email.)

JAIME *(in voice over)*
Dear Kurt:
I'm writing out of professional courtesy so that you do not feel somehow slighted by my search for another supervisor. As I mentioned in my email over a week ago, this research relationship is not working for me. Trying to complete my thesis from Central Australia with an inexperienced supervisor – no fault of your own – has been extremely distressing if not impossible, and I've had to make a hard decision – it's me or you. I don't want you to think this is a reflection of your obvious inability to supervise well, because I do appreciate what a difficult task this is, and how long it must take to develop these skills. You are a great musician and can be very supportive when not feeling threatened, and I wish you the best of luck. Thank you for all the great jazz you have turned me on to, but unfortunately I must go my own way. With warm regards, Jaime.

beat

KURT
FUCK!

(He paces for a minute. Finally, sits and opens the next email.)

NEIL SKINNER *(in voice over)*
Dear Kurt: What is going on down there? I'm writing to remind you that you are still on probation, and must seek better ways of resolving things with your students both in class and in supervision. Any attempt on your part to withdraw from this supervision relationship will reflect badly on your supervision record, which is currently non-existent, so I suggest you write a polite letter back to this student and

repair that relationship. If you need to go up to Central Australia to advise her effectively, or buy a Skype upgrade, I urge you to do so. Regards, Professor Skinner.

KURT
FUCK!!!

(He paces some more. Finally, sits and opens the next email.)

NEIL SKINNER *(again in voice over)*
Dear Jaime,
As the head of research in this faculty, I must advise you that it is not possible for you to drop a supervisor unless there is evidence of very serious infractions by that supervisor. This does not appear to be one of those cases. I urge you to do your best to repair things with Dr Smith-Whiteley. If you are unable to do so, and there is no formal complaint against him, you will lose your research place in this Faculty. I have every confidence that Kurt can provide you with expert supervision, and that you will jointly reach a very satisfactory conclusion between you to your current difficulties.
With warm regards, Professor Neil Skinner

ARRRRRGHGHHHHHHH!!!!!

(Pacing, deep breaths. Finally, he sits and begins to type.)

KURT
Dear Jaime
I have tried my best to address your concerns but obviously there are still some outstanding matters. Could you please email me your concerns and let's revisit our work together on resolving them? I'm happy to do this by email or skype. I have recently upgraded so that shouldn't be a problem. By the way, your presentation for the methods class is overdue now by twelve days and you are losing 5% per day.

I have cc'd Professor Skinner into this correspondence and hope to reach a satisfactory resolution soon. Kurt. Send. (*He hits a button but it doesn't send. He hits it again, harder.*) SEND!

(*There is a knock at the door. It catches him off-guard, obviously. MALCOLM stands in the open doorway.*)

KURT
Malcolm, sorry, come on in –

MALCOLM
Maybe you'd like a minute? I can come back –

KURT
No, no it's fine. I'm just having a challenging day.

MALCOLM
Anything I can do?

(*He sits down across from Kurt*)

KURT
No, I don't think so. It's just me, I – on the one hand I'm trying to write this biographical sketch for a book on 'innovative methodologies' and arts-based research, and then I get attacked by my nightmare student who – never mind, this is so boring – it's just me trying to get a handle on this crazy job. It's all a bit strange to me still and –

MALCOLM
Hmm. I wonder, does that mean you're not good at your job, or that you're better off somewhere else? Or maybe it means you're the one who can bring some change –

KURT
I'm not interested in bringing change. I just want to survive, and do work I like.

MALCOLM
(Laughs)
Isn't that what everyone wants? The great dream of the western world.

KURT
The great human dream!

MALCOLM
I guess so. To a point. For those who don't have to worry about cancer, starving, abuse, finding shelter for the night, protecting their children, whatever. What is it? Maslow, right?

KURT
Yeah, nice one. So, first world problems?

MALCOLM
More than that. I totally respect the fact that first world citizens like us have legitimate problems, I'm not saying that. But if a student comes to you with an anxiety disorder do you tell him to shut up and get on with it because someone else in the class broke their leg?

KURT
Well –

MALCOLM
No, you don't! They are both debilitating conditions for those two people. Your condition is debilitating too. And I respect that. But I'm just suggesting that maybe trying to fit in with the prevailing culture might not be the only, or even the best, strategy.

KURT
Is that what I'm doing?

MALCOLM
That's what you said. You want to learn the game and play it as a mechanism of self-protection.

KURT
I guess.

MALCOLM
It didn't help the Jews.

KURT
Excuse me?

MALCOLM
I'm Jewish by birth, and I refer to the Holocaust. There were plenty of Jews who just tried to assimilate and go along with the anti-Semitic changes that were occurring in 1930s Germany. They wrote about it too, in very similar words to yours – they just wanted to be left alone, wanted to figure out what was needed and do it, learn to be more strategic. But you know what? They were the first ones to die.

KURT
Oh great. Thanks for this little pep talk Malcolm, but –

MALCOLM
No, sorry! *Laughs*. What I'm trying to say is, trust you gut. Trust your gut, always trust your gut.

KURT
Thanks. What did you come to see me about?

MALCOLM
My gut.

KURT
Nice segue.

MALCOLM
I've been undergoing some – uh, treatment – and uh –

125

SCENE 7

KURT
Are you ok?

MALCOLM
Yeah, I'm okay. I just – it's having some side effects and I haven't been feeling very well, and I'm mindful that our next hurdle task for the methodology is due soon. Barb took us through Finding a Form last week.

KURT
I heard.

MALCOLM
Yeah. So, um – I'm thinking I'm going to be a bit late with that task. Would an extra week's extension work okay?

KURT
Of course, Malcolm, of course. Is there anything I can do to help?

MALCOLM
No, I'm – (*he gets a little emotional, pauses*) –

KURT
Malcolm?

MALCOLM
I'm okay.

KURT
Anything you want to talk about?

(*Beat*)

MALCOLM
No, not right now. I do appreciate the offer though. You know, I was in Allied Health for 37 years in one way or another. I know the power of the dialogue, there's nothing like it. And I believe

everything is relational – that's why I wanted to take this unit, as opposed to doing something with numbers and heavy theory and – I'm not interested in all of that. There's no relevance to my life at this stage. So I just wanted to say, thanks for running this unit.

KURT
Good, that's good. You're in the right place then.

MALCOLM
Yes, I believe so. But – I also want to say, about that finding your way through a career, or even a relationship or anything else for that matter, I just want to tell you … I mean, if I had a son I'd tell him to –

(He pauses again, overcome but not audibly crying.)

KURT
Malcolm –

(Long pause while Malcolm pulls himself together.)

MALCOLM
I'm just – working through some things. You know, when I was younger I was a musician too, a piano player. I loved playing piano more than anything. I was really good, and everyone in my small town – Deniliquin, do you know it? New South Wales – everyone in my town thought I'd be a famous rocker. I went for an audition at the Con in Sydney after high school, and it was awful. Humiliating. I was really bad, even I could see that. It was so crushing, on a consciousness level you know? Like going from being a big fish to a small fish overnight. Everyone was so gifted, *really* gifted. So there wasn't even anything to be angry about. And after that I just never felt THAT passionate about anything again. But when I found nursing and health services, especially palliative care, I loved it. Not like piano, but I loved it and I also loved that I could maybe help people a bit, give something back, which the piano thing didn't necessarily include.

But more importantly, I knew that if I didn't find something else to love again, I would become bitter and angry and empty and insufferable. And if end of life care teaches you anything, it teaches you that in the end it really doesn't matter what you do or what people think of it. What matters is whether it brings you joy, whether it takes you away somewhere, lets you reconnect to the beauty in life and overcome the overwhelming suffering that's everywhere we look. That's the most important thing. And you have that. I can see that you still have that. So don't give it away –

(Kurt is shocked and almost in tears. He nods. He just nods but his entire energy and embodiment has changed, relaxed, the anger is gone. He smiles weakly at Malcolm.)

MALCOLM
Thank you for the talk Kurt, I really needed that.
(He gets up to leave.)
Oh, and the extension too. Tell Barb I'll have it in next week. I appreciate it.

(He leaves and KURT packs up, heads to class)

(end of scene)

SCENE / CLASS 8: DOTTING THE I'S AND CROSSING THE T'S – RIGOUR OR RIGOR MORTIS?

(Kurt joins Barb in the classroom. They are waiting for the students to arrive. There is some undefined tension between the two. They both have their laptops out, more as a protection or a diversion than for actual work.)

BARB
Ok, who do we have first up?

KURT
Francine. Apparently, Francine's decided it's cool to be first to arrive these days.

BARB
I don't understand.

KURT
No, of course. Just a conversation Francine and I had over coffee a few weeks ago. She was perennially tardy and now look at her.

BARB
Fascinating.

KURT
Actually, it is. You know why Barb, because this unit turned her around. Sometimes the minutiae are important because it's a clue to genuine personal and social change. That's what ABR can do sometimes.
In my experience, anyway.

BARB
Fascinating.

KURT
Something bothering you Barb?

BARB
No. not at all.

KURT
Could have fooled me.

BARB
Something bothering you, Kurt?

KURT
Not a thing.
(under his breath) Not a fucking thing.

BARB
(inhales ready to launch into a response when Francine and Suzi appear together)
Ah Francine. On time I see.

FRANCINE
Yep. The new me.

KURT
Suzi do you want to grab a coffee in the staff room while you wait for your turn.

SUZI
We're together.

FRANCINE
Yes, we want to present together. We've come up with a proposal that brings our two ideas together in a really exciting way.

SUZI
Yeah, I really love it. We're both going to be performing.

BARB
It's really late in the semester to be changing directions.

KURT
Why don't we hear them out, Barb? Go on Suzi, Francine.

FRANCINE
It's not really a change of directions.

SUZI
We realised we were both working on the same idea, but with different stuff – what's the word, Francine, that you were talking about the other night?

FRANCINE
It's the same idea but we were working in different media. Now it's multimodal.

SUZI
Yeah, it's multimodal. We're both talking about women's identity – and how we express it – sometimes in difficult –

FRANCINE
– or inaccessible ways and modes.

SUZI
Yeah, so there are layers and the textures in sewing materials for the women in my building.

FRANCINE
And for mine, we want to create a layered and textured performance piece that captures the search for the women in my 'building' – which is actually the historical archive in my head.

SUZI
We think it'll work.

KURT
Are you working with the women in your apartment building Suzi? Are they all on board now?

BARB
I'm still quite concerned about the timeframe.

SUZI
We've got it under control Barb.

FRANCINE
Yep, we did a timeline – we've finished our interviews and we think we can finish the script in the next couple of weeks.

SUZI
My man is going to babysit the kids all day Saturday. That's heaps of time for me to work on this. Total luxury.

KURT
I think it sounds fantastic. It could be really groundbreaking.

BARB
I'm not entirely sure what you are going to be doing. What will your presentation look like?

KURT
What she means is –

BARB
I'm not trying to be negative; this is about rigour. I'm looking for where the research is and how it's going to be rigorous. Do you think you two can demonstrate that when you present … whatever it is you're going to present.

FRANCINE
It's going to be a performance. Like I originally planned. Only Dorothy is our muse, rather than our subject. I think she'd approve of the pillowcases that the women have been making. She lived in a Housing Commission flat at one point in her life, you know. She and these women have a lot in common. It's a way of bringing all their voices to life, and maybe to new audiences.

KURT
Did you know Dorothy Hewett was also a great cook? Maybe you can include a food element in the performance?

BARB
Honestly Kurt! I say just stay focused on your research topic, and on how your arts project relates to your research framework, and you should be fine. But you'll need to get a wriggle on.

FRANCINE
Thanks Barb. We've got it covered. We're having a blast.

KURT
Good on you Suzi, and you too Francine. Great initiative. Just email me – er, us – if you have any questions, or hit any road bumps in the next couple of weeks. Don't stay silent if you have a problem.

SUZI
Good advice Kurt.

FRANCINE
Thanks Kurt. We really think that bringing our two projects together have brought them to life. It happened organically and we just had to trust our instincts, like you told us.

SUZI
You're going to love it.

KURT
Well, good luck, and we'll see you next week. Check your email for the excursion location.

FRANCINE
Will do. Thanks Kurt, Thanks Barb –

SUZI
Yes, thank you.

(They leave together, excited. There is a tense silence in the room. Finally Kurt breaks the silence.)

KURT
I was just wondering Barb, if you have a creative bone in your body?

BARB
I beg your pardon.

KURT
Where's your creativity Barb? And your imagination? Could you have done any more to crush those women?

BARB
I don't think you've understood me at all.

KURT
You can say that again.

BARB
I'm not some fly by night fliberty jibbet. I'm doing my job here, making sure that the projects have structure and planning and a clarity of purpose.

KURT
Did you just say flibberty jibbert?

BARB
Do you see this?
(holds up large ring binder folder)
This is the university handbook. It's a legal document. We are legally obligated to ensure that what our students do complies with what is in the student handbook. And you can be as rude to me and irresponsible as you please, but it doesn't change what's in this book.

KURT
Please tell me you do not walk around with the university handbook.

(Barb starts to rise)

KURT
Okay, come on! What I'm saying is – what about what's in their hearts, and what they learn, *really* learn? From doing this work, from immersing in the high risk, unexpected learning that comes from putting yourself into the unknown?

BARB
Give it a rest Kurt. I've heard all of this before. I agree with about 80% of what you are saying.

KURT
Thank you.
(Kurt is interrupted by a knock on the door.)
Come in.

(Andrea appears in the doorway, with Gerard behind her, carrying his briefcase and his laptop as usual.)

ANDREA
Gerard and I are hoping to present together, so Gerard suggested I come to the consultation in his time slot. Is that ok?

(Kurt looks at Barb. Beat.)

KURT
It's a bit late to be changing your project folks.

BARB
Let's hear what you've come up with –

(Barb and Kurt exchange a softer if not amused glance)

GERARD
Should I go first Andrea?

ANDREA
Sure – why don't you outline the rationale we've formulated.

GERARD
Ok, I'll start and you bring it home? This is, um, this is, an *embodiment* of mixed methods research, where the researchers represent the content and the method. As a committed quantitative researcher, I *embody* (Gerard struggles with this word each time he has to say it) the position of the positivist paradigm, through presenting a graphic representation of quantitative data analysis – i.e. my survey results.

ANDREA
And …

GERARD
And as a principal, I represent and *embody* the experience of our target group and our key stakeholders, who are also principals.

ANDREA
(*in her excitement can't wait til Gerard finishes*)
– while I represent and embody the experiences of teacher and parent, the other two target groups and key stakeholders – and my presentation – sorry, my section of the presentation will employ arts-based methods – an art exhibition and ethnocinematic video of my whole school arts project: *Shakespeare lives in Yarra Junction*. Meaning I will co-create the video with my students, and it will be a mutual exploration of our differences and similarities – I'll be drawing on your work of course –

KURT
Are you sure you want to use ethnocinema? It's a big commitment you know, it's not an easy methodology –

ANDREA
I'm sure. I really love the principles and tools – and it just seems inherently pedagogical to me, so I want to give it a try.

KURT
Alright, well – it could be amazing, as long as you don't run out of time. Okay so just in case we've missed it – what's your research question again?

ANDREA
School Change

GERARD
School Change. It's always been school change. I think you'll recall my initial proposal dealt with some of the key literature around leadership and change.

ANDREA
You see, when Gerard and I got talking we realised we were both interested in finding ways to change the culture of schools – for the better. It was a bit of a light bulb moment for me, when Gerard starting going through some of the statistics from his pilot and I realised that his stats summed up my embodied, visceral experience as a teacher and a parent. So it was actually a no-brainer when we realised that.

GERARD
The mixed methods we selected were surprisingly compatible. I didn't think I'd be saying this, but the arts-based methods that Andrea suggested really complemented my own emergent findings.

ANDREA
Tell them Gerard …

GERARD
I even started keeping a video diary myself. I've been interested in video as a hobby for a number of years, so I had all the equipment I needed – it came to me quite easily!

ANDREA

Even if you do say so yourself. So, what do you think? Barb? You haven't said anything. We're not going to fail are we?

BARB

That's not at issue right now. As long as you meet the assessment criteria you should be fine. However, I'm not sure that your component could really be considered ABR, Gerard, and that's a key criterion for this task. Aren't you catching a ride on Andrea's methodology?

GERARD

But I thought our assignment would be regarded as whole, with complementary elements? That's how we've been approaching it.

BARB

Well, you've got another challenge on your hands. Think about how you can transform your data, Gerard – you have some building blocks, the video diary, and the parent video diaries

KURT

And all of that video equipment you have at home – I bet you have a home editing suite.

BARB

This is a big leap to take at this time in the semester, but I think you can do it. And I'm sure Kurt has faith in you, don't you Kurt?
(he nods)
This does raise some concern about the logistics and timing though. It sounds like a lot of data and maybe you are at risk of diffusing your focus?

GERARD

Actually we've talked about that, have we not, Andrea? I don't think it's an issue.

BARB
You certainly sound confident.

GERARD
Well I was until a minute ago.

KURT
Let's say we give them our blessing and send then on their way, Barb?

BARB
You don't need our blessing, you just need to cover the fundamentals, make sure all the ground work's been done and don't get too dazzled with the bells and whistles of your ABR methods, Andrea. The last thing you want is a project that is all smoke and mirrors, don't you agree?

(beat)

ANDREA
Good point, Barb. What do you think Gerard, is that what we're doing?

(beat)

GERARD
I think the last thing I'd ever be at risk of doing is turning my work into a circus act – not exactly my modus operandi, is it? And given the imperative, I'll concentrate on transforming that data as you suggest. I do believe we're on the right track. I think you'll find that we have laid the foundations, quite thoroughly. Andrea's done an excellent literature review and my analysis is thoroughly triangulated. Why don't you trust us and wait and see?

KURT
Let's not get carried away with the triangulation of data here, Gerard – you're still operating in a positivist paradigm. We deal with

multiple truths and provisional knowledge rather than proofs and validity. Take the leap into ABR – you're closer than you might think. *(pause)* You guys rock. I love the initiative and I can't wait to see what you make of Barb's challenge. Who knew you'd still be with us in Week 10 Gerard?

GERARD
Who knew? Well, we'll see you next week then. I presume the details of the excursion will be on the website.

KURT
Yep, and check your email as well, just in case there are any last minute changes.

GERARD and ANDREA
Thanks, bye.

BARB
Good luck.

KURT
See you next week.

(Andrea and Gerard leave. There is a long silence)

BARB
So, we're just waiting for Malcolm now.

KURT
(takes out his mobile)
I might give him a call. He was asking for an extension a few days ago, something about being crook for a while.

BARB
I thought he was looking a bit off colour in the last couple of weeks. *(surprised)*
Do you have his mobile number?

KURT
(*while waiting on the phone*)
Yeah, we've met for coffee a couple of times out of class. We were talking about going to a gig in Bennett's Lane – he plays piano. No answer. Didn't even go to message bank. He'll probably be here in a couple of minutes.

(*silence*)

BARB
You know, I think if you want to encourage your students to –

KURT
Please, no more advice, ok? I'm a bit – adviced out.

BARB
Fine, I'm just trying to help.

KURT
Believe it or not, I can see I have a lot to learn from you, but at the same time I come into this gig with years of experience playing and teaching in music, and no one seems to care. I'm just the new 'young gun' who somehow turned from an aging jazz saxophonist to a baby researcher – and I'm not a baby okay?

BARB
I know criticism is hard to take –

KURT
I've been taking criticism since I was 10 years old. The arts are *built* on criticism.

BARB
So is research. That's what we've got to help these students find out – the difference between arts and research.

KURT
I think the research part is the process between [the collaborators], or between us as collaborators in the classroom, or in the co-construction between audience and musicians or actors. What's different between art and research is – everything and nothing. Art *is* research, right? But –

BARB
They have a lot in common, sure. But are they the same? I've got an idea – why don't we teach the next session together?

KURT
But we just told them we are tag-teaming.

BARB
It's okay. They won't care. They won't even question it.

KURT
That's probably true, we'll be in the city on the graffiti excursion, right? Okay, let's do it.

BARB
Deal.

(end of scene)

SCENE / CLASS 9: MUSE OR MUSEUM? THEORY ON THE STREET

(BARB and KURT are lecturing in Hosier Lane with the class. GRAFFITI IMAGES are projected throughout the scene. The students are all taking pictures.)

BARB
Okay good morning everyone. I know it's hard to get out on a Saturday, so thanks for coming into the city.

KURT
Anybody need a coffee? Degraves Lane is just over there – world class coffee.

BARB
Can we get started please?

KURT
Sure. Go ahead Barb.

BARB
I've put together a bit of a treasure hunt for a few graffiti images here that I'd like you to walk around and find. Do you all have phones or other devices on you?

GERARD
I thought this was going to be a theory lesson.

BARB
Yes, it is. I'm taking another angle.

GERARD
Oh great, more innovation. You know I've got a lot on my plate with the assignment. I could have done with some more theoretical foundation.

ANDREA
Come on Gerard, you panic merchant, let's do it together.

FRANCINE
Go Barb – very hip!

(she winks, to which Barb does not respond)

BARB
So do you all have phones?

(murmurs of yes. Barb hands out a worksheet to each student)

BARB
Great. So when you find each station, you just look the keywords up online and get some background, make some notes … about what the references say and what you see for yourself.

MALCOLM
I'm afraid I might need some help with this one. But I do have a phone at least!

SUZI
I can help you. Dang, your phone's even older than mine, Malcolm.

FRANCINE
Can we do it in threes? I have a smartphone, guys.

BARB
Sure. Just as long as everyone gets the background. Go on and give it a try and –

KURT
– and let me guess, you'll go get a coffee?!

BARB
Funny Kurt. You're welcome to come.

(they cross the street for a coffee while the students start to find their way around the treasure hunt).

KURT
That was a really cool approach Barb.

BARB
Glad you approve. But why am I always the one doing theory?

KURT
Yes, why *are* you? What kind of coffee do you want?

BARB
(to the barrista)
Flat white please.

KURT
(to the barrista)
And a long black.
(to Barb)
It's cool to combine the theory with a street excursion like this but –

BARB
What?

KURT
Nothing, I was just – I was planning on doing some of this next week.

BARB
(glancing across to Hosier Lane, mindful that they should get back)
Let's go back and see what they are up to. I'm actually happy to do some theoretical unpacking –

KURT
Remember this is supposed to be you and me together. We talked about that the other day. So, you've done your opening bit with this

exercise, which is AWESOME, congrats, a great angle, I love it. But the rest is supposed to be us, and my bit is once they've reflected on what they've looked up to lead them in the differences between art and research. If there are any. Which I still feel ambivalent about. Are we still good with that?

BARB
Well, yeah, I – I just – if you want to revisit some of the earlier –

KURT
Let's stick with what we said, ok? I've got a good feeling about this. Come on –

(he takes his coffee and goes back to Hosier Lane)

KURT
How's it going over here – success?

FRANCINE
This is sooooo cool! Why aren't all our classes like this?

KURT
Just lucky I guess.

MALCOLM
We're struggling a bit.

KURT
Alright, how can I help?

MALCOLM
Well Suzi can't find all of the keywords because her spelling's not so great, and I can't see the goddamn screen because my eyes are not so great! What a pair.

SUZI
It's fun though – some of this artwork is unreal.

KURT
Okay well maybe we can make it fun AND possible.

(Barb joins, and approaches Andrea and Gerard)

GERARD
Barb, is it possible to have a bit more guidance here? I mean, what exactly are we looking for?

BARB
Have you been able to find the stations, and the keywords associated with them?

ANDREA
We found the stations, but maybe just not so sure how the keywords relate to the graffiti stuff on the wall is all. I don't get that.

GERARD
Well I certainly don't get it.

BARB
Okay, well let's look at this one. It's a small artwork by Banksy, see? Stop, take a good look. Now for the keywords 'Banksy Melbourne' – they take you to this article: *(projected)* http://www.smh.com.au/ entertainment/art-and-design/rats-two-more-banksy-artworks-lost-in-blunder-20130928-2uld0.html which talks about how this famous British graffiti artist's works are being painted over in Melbourne through anti-graffiti laws, and sometimes other tagging. So the first question at this station asks you to reflect on the difference between 'art' and 'vandalism'. The second question and our key question for this class, asks you to think about the relationship between art and research –

ANDREA
Why research?

BARB
Well what is the relationship between these important works being lost, and research?

ANDREA
No idea.

GERARD
Maybe if those people had done their 'research' – I'm using the term broadly, not academically – if these people had done their research then maybe those works wouldn't be lost?

ANDREA
Oh yeah. Okay, but at the end of that article, the owner of the rat building said that it's the nature of graffiti art to be lost. That's part of the deal. So how does that fit?

BARB
Good question. All good questions. That's exactly what we're wanting you to think about.

GERARD
Yeah but what's the answer?

KURT (joining in)
There is no answer.

ANDREA
Oh great. So why are we doing this?

BARB
There are *multiple answers.* That's what he means.

KURT
Oh yeah, that's what I meant! Thanks Ma.

BARB
It's a philosophical question but a practical one as well. Think about it, talk about it, try to avoid simplistic resolutions. No either/or's, ok?

SUZI (*approaches Barb & Kurt*)
Excuse me, but we are at station 3 and we're stuck.

(KURT & BARB look at each other, a silent negotiation)

KURT
Take it away Barb!

BARB
What's the problem Ajak?

SUZI
You can call me Suzi.

BARB
But Ajak is such a beautiful name!

SUZI
But I prefer Suzi for my Australian friends.

BARB
Am I saying Ajak wrong?

SUZI
No, I just prefer it –

KURT
Barb! (*makes a face like 'let it go'*)

BARB
What can we do for you?

SUZI

Well station three says we should find the difference between art that is outside on the street, and art that is across the street here at the National Gallery. I don't know what that means, and neither does Malcolm.

BARB

It's asking you to consider the possibility that where the artwork is PLACED makes it look different, feel different, or is seen differently by you.

SUZI
(Still confused but doesn't want to say)
Okay. Yep. I'll tell Malcolm.

(she walks away)

KURT
Barb did you come up with this activity yourself?

BARB
What are you implying Kurt?

KURT
(laughs)
No, I'm just wondering. It's so –

BARB
It's so what Kurt? So young? So cool? So hip that it couldn't possibly be my idea? I was teaching interactively before you were even BORN my friend –

KURT
I'm sure. Of course. And your son had no input whatsoever?

(beat. She relaxes – they laugh together)

BARB
My son, dammit. It's good though, right?

(they laugh some more. Suddenly, Suzi comes running)

SUZI
Help, help Malcolm's not well. He looks funny and he can't talk.

(They all run over. Malcolm is sitting on the ground, looking grey)

BARB
Malcolm? What are you feeling?

MALCOLM
I'm okay. I'm –

KURT
Let's get you up –

BARB
No! Leave him. Somebody run across the street and get some water.

(Andrea goes)

MALCOLM
(a bit better now, breathing a bit easier)
I'm okay. Just a spell.

BARB
That was more than a spell Malcolm. Do you want me to call a doctor?

MALCOLM
No, thanks. I've been ill and – I guess I'm just a bit weak still. Sorry for the drama, I –
(he grabs the wall again to steady himself)
I'll just sit here for a minute.

KURT

How about we all head over to DeGraves for a coffee together? I had a debrief activity planned – no reason why we can't do that with a good strong latte? What do you think Malcolm?

MALCOLM

Good idea. You go on ahead and I'll join you all in a tick – just need to catch my breath.

SUZI

I'll wait with you Malcolm.

(All leave, except Malcolm and Suzi. End of scene.)

INTERMEZZO 5: BETWEEN A ROCK
AND A HARD PLACE

(Kurt in his office, pacing, then goes back to his computer where he is in the midst of a skype call with Jaime. We can hear Jaime's responses but can't see her on the projected computer screen.)

KURT
Jaime? Could you come back and finish this please? This isn't how Skype is supposed to work. I talk, then you talk, then I talk etc etc. Could you please hang up and talk to me.

JAIME
I'm done. Just had to sort out some filming for the morning. There's this young Indigenous kid who's discovered video big time, and he's totally into the ethnocinema angle. He's my new DOP. We've got some incredible footage of each other already – it's so beautiful, I can't believe all ethnographic film isn't using –

KURT
You're kidding right? We've been through this oh, I don't know, about twenty times. Jaime, you CAN'T start filming til your ethics amendments are through.

JAIME
Why can't you support me, Kurt? Why am I stuck with the one supervisor in the whole faculty who doesn't understand how to meet a student's needs? I think I'm doing something really important up here and you block me at every turn. Why did you even bother to set up this skype if you didn't want to really talk to me?

KURT
(about to explode, but takes a deep breath, pauses to control himself before speaking)
Jaime, Jaime, stop. … It's not about me, it's about your study.

JAIME
Well, that's a first.

KURT
After the hours and hours we spent going through your proposal, and your methodology, and your insecurities, and your paranoia, and your passions, and well, god knows what else we covered in those meetings. How could you be complaining about me – again?

JAIME
You really don't know, do you?

KURT
Enlighten me. Please.
(long pause, Kurt looks at the screen, starts working on his keyboard)
Jaime? Are you still there? I've lost vision.

JAIME
I turned it off. You led me on Kurt.

KURT
What?

JAIME
You toyed with my feelings.

KURT
I? I toyed with your feelings? Are you kidding me? You know I'm –

JAIME
You made me feel like I could do anything, conquer the world. You made me feel like I could come up here, and be brilliant. Be the Jean Rouch of Central Australia and it was nothing like that. It was dirty and difficult and hot and no-one would talk to me, not one person till I met Jake. I felt like a complete fraud and it was embarrassing. All

those meetings before we left, you made me feel smart, and powerful, and attractive. You were my muse, my inspiration.

KURT
You do know I'm gay, don't you? I have a partner, Tom. He's at home right now, probably wondering where the hell I am, again. I'm gay, Jaime. I am not interested in you in any way.

JAIME
This was never about sex, Kurt! It was much more than that, it was about me – the person and believe me, I know that you are not interested in me, now. You've made that perfectly clear by not answering my emails or my phone calls.

KURT
This is harassment.

JAIME
You can talk about harassment! Don't you speak to me about harassment, Kurt. Playing with my feelings is the worst possible kind of harassment, and that's what I've outlined in my email to Professor Skinner.

KURT
What are you talking about?

JAIME
Well, he wouldn't let me change supervisors without a good reason, so I gave him one. A nice big fat juicy reason.

KURT
For gods sake Jaime. Are you serious? Look, why don't you come down to Melbourne for the final class like we talked about earlier. You can present on your proposal – you could show some footage. We could call it a pilot study – I'll get it past Barb somehow.

JAIME

You have no idea Kurt. What you did to me. I believed in you totally. I wanted to be just like you – the hip cool muso who could also be an academic. You made me think that was possible.

KURT

I don't know what you are talking about. Seriously.

JAIME

Our relationship was the most important thing in my life.

KURT

We don't have a relationship. I'm just your supervisor – the poor schmuck who got to meet with you at your every whim, ferret out every reading I thought you might be able to handle, and now gets to stay late Skyping when I should be home having dinner with my partner.

JAIME

You shouldn't be in that job Kurt. You really need to find another line of work.

(Sound of Skype call being ended.)

KURT

Jaime? That's not what I meant. I don't want to be anybody's role model. Oh god, give me a break, would you please?

(Kurt pulls out his mobile phone and dials.)

KURT (continued)

Hi Babe. Are you home yet? Are you pissed off? Please don't be pissed off with me, I couldn't bear it. Having a shitty day. Look, don't wait dinner for me. I'll grab something here. Something urgent's come up and I have to sort it right now.

(Kurt ends the call, fishes in his backpack and finds an apple at the bottom of the bag. He begins to eat his apple, staring into space, immobilized. SWITCH TO other side of stage where:

Barb is sitting in her office in an old armchair. She has a desk with several piles of folders, with a pin board behind it. Each pile, each of differing heights, has a label – Administration, Ethics, research projects, supervision, new grant applications, Barb, teaching, ABR class. Apart from the piles, laptop and phone, the desk is clear. There is a lamp in the corner, switched on – it's evening. Barb is on the phone. She has a manila folder in her lap.)

BARB
Hi Kurt, call me back, would you? It's Barb. Tonight if possible. I'm at the office for another hour. Thanks.
(hangs up, goes back to reading folder. She digs a muesli bar out of her bag. Pause, chews, hits redial and waits through answering machine message.)
You're not going to answer your phone are you? Why would you be the only Gen Xer who doesn't have his phone surgically implanted – *(into the machine again)* – Oh, hi Kurt, me again. I'm not stalking you, and I know it's only an hour since I saw you at class but I think we really need to talk. I've just received this email from the Dean. I think you know what I'm talking about, it's the … Shit.
(dials again, waits)
Hi Kurt, I need to talk to you about Jaime. Oh hi, yes. I didn't expect live Kurt. How are you? … Yes I know it's only been an hour but – yes, I've had an email from the Dean … Dean Skinner, yes, about Jaime … Well, it's awkward … You know what it says … I'd prefer if it wasn't my business, but he's is still insisting I get involved, he's put it fair and square in my lap. And he's just sent me Jaime's last email.

… Kurt … Kurt … yes … Yes … Yes, I understand that … Maybe not as well as you but I do have a certain amount of empathy … can we please not bicker, this is important. Kurt, you're in trouble … It doesn't matter …. It really doesn't matter, you can't let a student go

off the rails like that. What were you doing approving her trip to Alice Springs .... Yes it was your call. ... You did sign off on it, I have the paper work in front of me ... She's the student, that's why. It's not in her interests to be that unsupervised, or yours ... I know she's very bright, I can see that from her emails .... She's obviously very creative, and deluded. Or something ... honestly, I'm not judging you Kurt, I want to help you save your job .... Yes, I'm serious, this could bring you undone .... Well, she's contravened the code of ethics for one thing .... You actually can't do that when you're covered by university ethics ... that's the whole point of having the *protocol* .... No, she can't make her film in those camps without the permission of the people she's filming. No, it doesn't matter if it's fictionalized, the people still have to give their permission .... Pseudonyms don't make them any less identifiable, it's a film for gods sake. Can you please talk to her .... Get her on a plane home .... Whatever you have to do .... Sorry, what did you say? ... Jaime said what? ... Oh shit, you're kidding me. No this is serious, just go home Kurt. Come and see me in the morning and we'll think of something. Okay, take care.
(hangs up, looks even more concerned.)
Shit, Kurt. Really?
(head in hands)

(end of scene)

SCENE/ CLASS 10: CONTESTED TERRITORIES. WHEN BLURRING THE BOUNDARIES MEANS CROSSING THE LINE

(The classroom: desks have been organized neatly into rows and there is a new electronic whiteboard installed since the students were last in the room. The overhead projector is nowhere to be found. The scene opens with all students except Malcolm seated. Barb and Kurt are both standing up addressing the students, although it is not initially clear whether this is the class, or parallel interior monologues.)

BARB
First, 'do no harm' –

KURT
'Do no harm' – yep, do no harm, whatsoever.

BARB
When we talk about ethics in research, whether it's arts-based research, ethnography or statistics, the ethos should be the same – first, do no harm.

KURT
Let's talk about what 'harm' means, just for a minute. Who's going to get hurt when you make a piece of art? Who's harmed when Banksy pulls on his balaclava and whips out his aerosol can and does his thing in Hosier Lane at 2 am some summer morning? No, seriously, who's that going to hurt?

BARB
I really want to say, no-one, because I love what Banksy represents – I am both confronted and compelled by his work – by his anonymity and his originality. I wanted to say that I was not quite convinced about his contribution to research, but I realized that this was shortsighted of me. I believe every work he creates and locates is a

question, an inquiry, a creation of new knowledge – and not just him, but many of the street artists we looked at in the last class.

But no harm? As unfashionable as it is to say this: what about the landowners, who didn't choose to have street art on their walls? What if they had a different aesthetic, planned a different design for their exterior wall? Sure, it's unlikely, but is it some anonymous, random artist's right to make that decision, or to take that decision away from the person who owns the wall? What if the work is offensive in some way? What if it's not Banksy, but some wannabe, and the art is bad? Is there still no harm?

KURT
Isn't it the artist's responsibility to challenge, to confront, to create new knowledge by turning over the status quo and dispatching it to oblivion? Pushing – all the time, pushing the boundaries, maybe not saying please and thank you, and are you okay I hope I didn't harm you, but –

BARB
You may be right Kurt.

KURT
I think so.

BARB
And if that's what you really, genuinely think, then you probably, one hundred per cent, shouldn't be working at a university. You're dangerous.

KURT
I take that as a compliment.

BARB
I'm sure you do. I'm sure you go home and celebrate every time you break the rules, subvert the order, encourage a student to take their work just that little bit further than might be safe. And you know

160

what happens then Kurt? Other people pick up the pieces. Because being an artist who is also a researcher working in 'the academy' doesn't give you the right to invade someone's privacy or betray a confidence or put a person's most intimate details on show without their permission, or send a student to Alice Springs to make culturally inappropriate videos with impunity, and do you know why? Because it's not ethical. We're legally bound.

KURT
Well how the hell are we ever going to climb Mt Everest if we don't take a risk? Or find the cure for the stomach ulcer if we don't trial it on ourselves? It's uncomfortable, and difficult and sometimes totally terrifying to be at the cutting edge, but that is not only what good art has always done Barb, it's what good research has too. And it's terrifying, and sometimes dangerous, yes it is.

Not that you'd know anything about that Barb. You haven't left suburbia for years. Nice safe, dot the I's, cross the T's, look both ways before you step off the curb, and pick up your swollen paycheck on your way out the door – Barb. Chairperson of the, you guessed it, the ethics committee. And how's that working out for you? You are bored out of your ever-loving mind. And pissed off. So pissed off you take it out on me, the one person in this whole damned university who might just give you a ticket out of that stultifying little world you've built for yourself in Ethics Committee Land.

BARB
You don't know the first thing about me. Or about the choices I've made. Or the sacrifices. If I'm so goddam straight and stuffy, how come I'm the one, the only one in this faculty pulling for you Kurt. How come it's me, boring, middle-aged, conservative, pissed off Barb who saved your job today? Tell me that.

KURT
Don't be ridiculous. My job isn't on the line from some crank student like Jaime. And anyway, even if it was, you're the last person I'd ask to save it for me. I couldn't bear to be … obligated.

BARB
You're a child. You think Skinner decided to back off on the Jaime business because you asked him nicely? You think it's okay to say exactly what you think, when you think it, to impressionable 25 year olds because you're inconvenienced by the crush they have on you? Where have you been living Kurt, because it sure as hell hasn't been on planet Earth. Grow the hell up. Here, take my notes for tonight's class – you can do the lot – you don't even have to acknowledge your sources – just tell the students, when they get here, that I'll be available for consultations for their projects all next week – can you do that much for me, Kurt?

(She goes to leave)

ANDREA
We're right here.

FRANCINE
We've been here the whole time.

GERARD
And frankly, it's getting a bit old. So you don't see eye to eye –

SUZI
So what. You've got nothing on me and my old man. Now him, that's something to complain about.

FRANCINE
You realize you have more in common than you have differences? Do you want to advance arts-based research or not? It seems like you'd rather just get bogged down in your different approaches. Such a waste –

ANDREA
Yeah come on. We're all on the same team here, right? At least you two are, if you could just stop arguing and recognise it. And I've got

empirical evidence for it. I've been writing about you in my journal since Week One.

GERARD
Actually, so have I. I've done a statistical analysis and a discourse analysis. I have it here on my computer.

FRANCINE
We haven't got time Gerard. I actually want to continue with ethics. I'm really struggling with a question about dependent relationships and want to talk about it – tonight.

(Kurt and Barb look to each other to see who will respond first, and how.)

FRANCINE
Dependent relationships?

ANDREA
What about transparency?

FRANCINE
What about trustworthiness?

KURT
Barb?

BARB
I think there's something to be said for trustworthiness … in research.

KURT
And in artistic collaborations. Try playing jazz with people you don't trust. You'd never go anywhere new.

BARB

Why don't you talk a bit more about that? Have you got an example, from your career? Your other career?

KURT

I've got a doozy, but it's not from my career. Who's heard of a book called *The Sneaky Kid*? Now there's an ethics story. If this had come up in Barb's ethics committee they'd all have been taken off in ambulances.

(Barb laughs out loud – perhaps for the first time? Everyone is shocked.)

BARB

That's probably true. Tell them –

KURT

So, Harry Wolcott. Where to start. The ethics of arts-based research and harm. I think I have a handout, yes Barb, a handout – this is a scene from Johnny Saldana's play, I think we should read it together.

(As Kurt is shuffling through his backpack looking for the handouts, Malcolm enters. He is clearly unwell and quite agitated)

KURT

Hey Malcolm.

FRANCINE

You picked a bad night to be late – we've just watched the first two acts of *Who's Afraid of Virginia Woolf.*

BARB

And some of us are a little mortified. So far in this class I've had a first class meltdown and now a slap down drag out with another staff member. What is it about ABR that brings out the worst in me?

KURT
Did you ever consider that maybe there's a reason for that.

BARB
Like maybe I shouldn't be here?

KURT
Or like, maybe you should. Maybe this brings you close to stuff you've jammed in a bottom drawer for a long time.

BARB
A shed, actually.

FRANCINE
Excuse me George and Martha, could we move on. What's up Malcolm? Can't you find a seat? There's one over there near Suzi.

MALCOLM
(goes to the seat at the front near Suzi and sits on the desk)
The garden's not finished. I bought ten yellow roses, just small ones, at Bunnings a week and a half ago, some dynamic lifter and some mulch, and some of that tan bark that they dye black so that it doesn't look like tan bark. But I haven't planted the roses. It's Marian's birthday next month and I was doing it for her. She could look out the window and see these roses, beautiful perfect yellow roses – from me – to remind her of me, and I haven't finished preparing the soil. I can't put them in until it's all turned over, and rested and the earth worms are doing their thing. And I'm out of time. Well, that's what they tell me. Time's up. But it can't be. I'm not done, not by a country mile.

KURT
Malcolm?

(they all exchange looks of concern)

MALCOLM

I've been working on the presentation for Week 12 and it's not quite right. It's still ... unresolved, everything is unresolved. I keep asking a question with the artefacts that represent the people I've interviewed but the artefacts aren't speaking back. They remain inanimate objects, devoid of art and meaning. They just sit there, silent. And when I take up one object and ask it, 'what can you tell me about the life of the person who chose you to represent them?', it is silent. Silent. So you see, I have to be patient. Not be **a** patient. I have to wait until the object is ready to give up its answer, to reveal its meaning to me, so that I can reveal it to you. These things can't be rushed. And, I'm out of time.

It just doesn't seem fair, does it? That I should have to wait for a rock to speak. I kid you not, one of them chose a rock and told me that this was the object which best captured an essence of them. Do you think they were having a lend of me? I could go back and ask that woman what she meant when she gave me that rock, but I can't. Because, you see, she died last week. She was a patient, and she was a participant in my project, and she was my friend. Am I blurring ethical lines here? And she was my mirror. My god, what am I saying? I'm talking to a bunch of strangers about the most intimate details of my life, well, what's left of it, and I haven't given ten minutes of intimacy to Marian in the last five months. How could I be so selfish?

I'm sorry, I have to go, I have to put the roses in, Marian's waiting. I'm not sure if I'll be back. It's been wonderful – you're all wonderful. Good luck to you all ...

(he rushes out.)

(end of scene)

SCENE 11: CLASS NOTES

KURT

First do no harm. Where do I begin? I was so sure that was a crock of shit. In my sleep I dream of improvising, of glorious riffs where there is no thought, only feeling. No analysis, only the body. When I wake up, I think, I can't remember how to improvise. Well, obviously, there is no remembering, only doing. I have to start playing again. And I have to get on a plane to Alice. Somehow, Jaime, you and I need to find the bridge.

BARB

Tonight I told Kurt he had no business being at a university and he told me I belonged – here, in an ABR class, with these students, with Malcolm. I do believe it's the other way around. This is his place. He needs it. Maybe he doesn't know that yet, but there is something waiting for him here, if he can find a way to let the past be. He is not lesser, being here. But I am. I am diminished – I diminish myself. I lock the past in the shed and refuse to let it breathe. It suffocates in that neglected place. If I am to be ethical, I do believe I cannot do ethics any more.

ANDREA

I have roses in my garden. They're blooming at the moment. I feel guilty at the pleasure they bring me. I know what he's talking about, the ground must be prepared or the roses just don't grow right. No point in putting them in until the earth has been invaded by the worms. Timing is everything, and everything takes too much time – gardening, love, art, research. Oh Malcolm, it's too much to bear.

GERARD

I didn't realise he was sick. I didn't realise it was anything serious. How much am I missing? How much do I miss at work, in life –? How many Andreas have I missed before, how much could be different if I could only really believe in multiple ways of knowing?

FRANCINE

Why does it always turn out that the real truths come from the most unexpected places? If you had asked me in the beginning who would teach me the most in this class about arts-based research, I don't think any of us would have chosen Malcolm. Is that the common thread between art and research – the unexpected? Making the familiar strange? These strangers have become familiar, and I – I know now that for me, art and research both begin in *desire*, not in a question. They begin in the guts, not in the mind. They begin in a *wanting*, not in a *knowing*. This work is too hard without deep deep unquenchable desire.

SUZI

I am completely alone. My days are crowded with people and yet I can reach no-one. The children, their father, the women who I sew with, they all buzz around me, making noise, asking things of me. And I give over, my time, my attention, but not my heart. That I keep to my self. Malcolm gives over his heart, even to me, and he doesn't even know me. I'm going to keep sewing. I'm going to make a video of the women, sewing. For Malcolm, for me, for all of us.

(end of scene)

SCENE / CLASS 12: CRITICAL PLAYS

(Kurt and Barb are sitting in the classroom in silence. Andrea, Francine and Suzi sit in one corner whispering to one another. Barb is marking papers, and Kurt sits staring into the distance. Gerard walks in late. They all look up eagerly, then – almost disappointed – acknowledge Gerard.)

KURT
Hey Gerard.

GERARD
Sorry I'm late –

BARB
You're fine.

ANDREA
Hi Gerard, come sit here.

GERARD
(he does)
Is Malcolm back?

ANDREA
(quietly)
No –
(They get into undertone whispered conversation – Andrea and Suzi are catching him up.)

BARB
To Kurt
Should we start?

(He doesn't respond. He is upset.)

BARB

Tonight is our chance to reconnect with one moment, one act, one possibility.

Tonight we get to need each other.

Tonight we get to love a student.

Tonight Malcolm gets to have risk.

Tonight we get to transcend risk.

Because we have somehow, suddenly, or messily over time, become a family, a community, a collaborative team doing risky business, and I was wrong when I said do no harm. But I was right by the university. I was being professional. Ethical? I DON'T want to do harm – but it's an ideal, right? It's an ideal that can lock us into a woollen closet and kill the best of what we have to offer.

SUZI

What is harm? That's what I don't get. You talk about this shit like it's obvious, I swear to god, it's ridiculous how you people think you know what everyone wants and deserves and gets. See, black people don't make stupid rules like 'do no harm', black people are like 'don't kill me first' because we're used to harm, we expect it. You don't even know how white you sound! Seriously. I hope Malcolm is ok, he's a nice man and we need him in here.

ANDREA
To Gerard
I thought he was looking better, didn't you? I mean, I knew something was wrong, but I never knew it was a terminal diagnosis, and I certainly never thought it was imminent. I think we should go and see him. I mean, what is the point of this 'arts-based research, real world research' if we can't use it to do something small and full of love for one of our own?

GERARD

What if he doesn't want visitors Andrea, what if he doesn't want anyone to know? He CHOSE not to tell us, right? I mean, he's a pretty articulate guy, he's an *end of life carer* for god's sake, and he's on pretty friendly terms with Kurt too, so I think if he wanted us to know he would have told us.

FRANCINE
Okay, you have TOTALLY just missed the point of this entire unit.

GERARD
Oh have I? Why don't you enlighten me –

FRANCINE
No, I mean – sorry, I'm just saying that this whole unit is about how we can all use ABR in our own lives to transcend WORDS, right? I mean, how we don't learn by words, we don't generate new knowledge with WORDS alone, right? But with actions, with doing –
(To Kurt and Barb)
Isn't that what you've been modelling for us? I mean, for all we know, you are the best of bloody friends! The way I take it, you've been modelling creative tension for us this whole time. You are showing us how words just always come up short, and actions must be organic, collaborative, grounded in our own experience, time and place. And are NOT measurable by simple rubrics, essays or whatever – isn't that what Eisner was on about? Not measuring apples like oranges? I mean, that's what I thought you've been saying. Have I missed the point?

KURT
(Visibly moved)
No, you haven't. You have gotten it completely. Better than us –

BARB
You know Francine, that was perfect. That is all we've ever wanted you people to think about, to debate, to know in your minds and bodies.

SUZI
We know it.

FRANCINE
We do! We know it. We talk about it all the time. I thought you knew that. We have a Facebook page for this class.

(KURT looks at Barb, Barb looks at Kurt. They smile? Connect.)

BARB
Should we – talk about next week, or discuss your projects?

ANDREA
Yes, let's go around the room and say where we are up to. I know I'm a little nervous about next week – it's our last class, right? I'm a little nervous.

FRANCINE
Can we talk about Malcolm please? First?

KURT
Sure.

GERARD
Has anyone been in to see him?

KURT
I have. He's very weak.

FRANCINE
What do you mean? Is h – is it temporary?

BARB
I think we should –

KURT
No one knows.

BARB
Is everyone okay to talk about this? Because it might be upsetting to some –

SUZI
If you are talking about me, I have seen more death than you will ever dream of. So don't worry about me. I'm how do you say it? "Intimately acquainted".

(beat)

FRANCINE
Is he going to make it?

KURT
No, he's not going to 'make' it, no. But I don't know if this is his last round either. He is very weak, and he's getting some drugs and says he's feeling better than that night last class, but it's hard to tell. I think he's lost more weight even since then and –

BARB
How are you all feeling?

GERARD
We should go see him.

KURT
Has anyone else been?

ANDREA
No, we wanted to respect his privacy.

BARB
Yes, and I think that's a very good impulse –

KURT
He wants visitors. I mean, he has a big family and I know they are most often there. But he's got a lot of people in his life, like any teacher, and he loves the visits. He has been happy for distractions, so I think he'd love a visit.

BARB
But we can't PRESUME –

KURT
No, but we can ask him.

SUZI
I'm going to visit him.

FRANCINE
I'll come with –

GERARD
You can't just walk in there –

SUZI
Why not? This is a free country, right?

GERARD
Well if you're going, we should all go. Let's go together.

ANDREA
Do we even know what is actually wrong with him? Kurt, do you know?

BARB
He has cancer. He has terminal liver cancer, and he did this class to leave something reflective behind for his family. He didn't want us to know.

(There is silence. Kurt looks stricken.)

SUZI
He's a good man. Strong.

FRANCINE
Strong sure, but everyone needs support. I say we go whether he wants us to or not. Come on, he would not have taken this class if he didn't want to deal with this terrible diagnosis. We are his community, that's what ABR has given us – we have to go!

KURT
What if we have the presentations there? If he's still there next week? Then he can still be part of it –

BARB
I think we'd have to get permission from him, or his wife or –

KURT
Obviously. But if he wants it, what do others think?

FRANCINE
I think it would mean the world to him!

SUZI
Yep, totally. Plus, I'd rather present my final project to him, with him in the group, that's all.

ANDREA
Yeah, me too! I'm in.

GERARD
Well it has to be up to Malcolm, doesn't it?

BARB
Yes it does. It sure does. We'll check it out with Malcolm.

(They all kind of simultaneously look at Kurt, who is so choked up he cannot speak.)

BARB

How about we take a 10 minute coffee break, and come back to review final problems or questions with your projects?

(They all leave except Kurt. Barb sits, unresolved about what to do, as Kurt begins to speak.)

KURT

He's like a father to me. I know that's bad, not having boundaries but –. I love him, he was helping me understand things, and now he's just – going! When we've just met.

BARB

It's okay. We'll go see him. He loves you too, Kurt, that's obvious. And you gave him something back, you know? You gave him an incredible gift.

(She hugs him, and Kurt lets her.)

(end of scene)

SCENE 13: CODA

BARB

(evening, Barb is working through the ethics folder, stops, picks up the phone)

… Hi Jono, it's Mum, call me back.

(hangs up. Pause. picks up phone again)

Hi Jono, I'm not stalking you honestly, just wanted to catch up. It's been a while. Call me.

(hangs up; picks up phone)

Hi honey, do you remember that trip we took up to the Scottish highlands when you were nine? I was just thinking about it and I couldn't help wondering if you remembered that little town we stayed on the coast, with Skye in the distance? Dad and I took you to all those places we'd been before you were born, when I was on that research trip, doing the fieldwork for my PhD? For some reason it's been coming back to me a lot lately. I had this memory of you, on the beach, nine o'clock at night, helping to build a bonfire with the local kids. What a night that was. There was something about that place, something mystical, primal. You were just a little kid, but did you feel it? Did you know what I did that summer? I haven't told anyone this. I was on study leave to finish that book on qualitative methodologies, and I didn't write a word. I painted, I wrote character studies of the blokes down at the local hotel, and I even started a novel only a couple of chapters – long lost now, historical, all my research on ceilidhs flowed into that bit of writing. I wonder what the hell happened to that –

Hello? Hello? Is this still running? Bloody hell Jono, just delete this – I'm obviously completely mad. Actually just procrastinating. I've got to chair the ethics committee in the morning, and honestly, I'd rather be talking to you, even if you're not there. Where are you by the way? Talk to soon. Love you. You know this is Mum right? Of course you do. I'm a hanging up now.

SCENE 13

(Kurt's office: Kurt is sitting staring into space, eating an apple. He takes out his mobile phone and dials.)

KURT

Hi babe, it's me again … No, not on the tram yet … Yeah I know I said I'd be home early but something's come up and it's urgent … I don't always say that …. I don't! Look, I'll cook tomorrow night, okay? I'll do that laksa you love, promise. Don't be mad. … No, I'm fine …. Yep, just have to sort out some admin with a couple of students. What can I say, it's assessment week … Okay, just leave it in the pot. I'll warm it up … love you, bye.

BARB

(Later, almost all the folders have been removed from the desk. The office is completely cleared, except for the phone, and the ABR pile of folders. Phone in hand, Barb waits.)

Whatever you do, don't answer the phone Kurt, why change the habit of a – Oh, hi it's Barb here, give me a call when you get this message. I need to talk to you about assessing the ABR class. How are we going manage these exegetical folios? I know we've discussed it but I was wondering if you had a *(message tape cuts out)* – shit – rubric.

(picks up phone, dials)

Hi Malcolm, how are you? Can you talk? … So you're doing ok? Really? … Great, that's great. Thanks for letting us come by and do the presentations for you. It means a lot to the group. Don't worry about your final piece, just now. We can sort it later. You've made such significant contribution to the class already. Such as what? Well, I don't really have to tell you, do I. They've all grown so much. Look at Suzi – yeah, Suzi and Francine working together, nearly as surprising as Gerard and Andrea. They're positively formidable. Yes, Kurt's ok. Yep, he's a force of nature. Like a hurricane. Kidding.
(laughs)

178

Me? … It's funny you should say that. I have been doing that very thing. How did you know? I only read that one piece, that was ages ago. I've been thinking about something new. I think it's time. I don't know Malcolm, I'm world-weary. Terrible thing to say to you, under the circumstances. I've got to tell you, something's happened over these past weeks. Each time I've come into that class and listened to the students, to you, talking about the projects you're working on, it's hard to describe, the lights are on and everyone is home. Everyone is so, connected to what they're doing, even Gerard – especially Gerard who discovered his inner artist at the eleventh hour. What is it that Barbara Myerhoff says? 'Thinking with my viscera, feeling with my brain', learning from all my history and hunches and senses …?

Every week I'd come back to my office, sit down at the pile of papers on my desk, eat a muesli bar, and wonder what the hell I was missing. And then, one night, I was out of muesli bars, the system was down, the phone was out, and I thought I was in heaven. Sorry Malcolm … I'm just running off at the mouth. I really only called to see how you were doing … Sure … No problem. What? Oh, I'm thinking I might travel. Not sure, maybe Scotland … You think? … Ok Malcolm, I'll tell them. Anyway, you'll be seeing them yourself on Tuesday. You take care now. See ya. … Yep … Bye.
(she hangs up, pauses.)

KURT
(Kurt picks up the landline, checks his computer screen for a number and dials)
Hi! Malcolm! It's Kurt. How are you man? Yeah? … that's good … great …
Well I just wanted to give you a call to let you know that, you know, you don't need to worry about the presentation assessment. Take as long as you need. Yes, of course, I understand that too. You wouldn't want to leave it too long. … You could give us a call when you're discharged. We could get the class together – I think they'd like to do that. You wouldn't believe it but they're a tight group these days. Even Gerard …

Me? Fine ... no really, I'm fine Malcolm. ... just a bit of a bureaucratic shitstorm – you know better than most. Some days I think I'd be better off hitting the road again with the band – that'd be a sight to see, five geriatric musicians pumping out the tunes at some Leagues Club on the Gold Coast. ... Anyway, that ship's sailed. Sorry man, I shouldn't be complaining to you of all people ... You do? You think I could do that? ... She said what? ... Bullshit. She thinks I'm incompetent. *(beat)* Well that's nice of you to say Malcolm. You know, I've been bitching a lot about this course, but I love it. And I think I could be good at it ... If Jaime doesn't sue me or Skinner doesn't fire me ... I think I could, I don't know, light some fires. Open some new doors: art meets life meets knowledge. It could be a blast.

Wow, listen to me! Now who's gone over to the dark side? Don't tell anyone I'm actually getting excited about academia. It might damage my rebel reputation. And for god's sake don't tell Barb. If she knew I was lining up to work with her again next year she'd probably have a stroke – Malcolm? Are you all right?

I'd better let you get some rest. See you next week, okay. Don't worry about the extension. Take as long as you need. Hey Malcolm, how would you feel if we held the class in your room at the – okay I'll say it, hospice. Everyone wants to see you. We all miss you.
(beat)
Okay, great. Thanks but let's see how you're feeling on Monday. I'll check in with you then. Yep, see you then.

(He hangs up. CUT TO:)

(The classroom is as it was for Class 1. It is empty. The fancy new whiteboard /projector is on a rolling slide show of images from Malcolm's project. The door opens and Jaime, carrying her backpack and her laptop and video camera round her next, enters.)

JAIME
Kurt? Hello, any one here?

(takes our her mobile phone and dials – voicemail picks up)
Hi Kurt, it's Jaime. I'm here to do my presentation. Is this class happening or what?
(irritated, she hangs up, and notices the slideshow. Sits to wait, and watches.)

MALCOLM
(in voice over)
Thanks for coming by, and sorry if I'm not here to share presentations with you. But I do have something to share anyway. I want to tell you what I've learned over these past weeks. I'm not sure if you remember this, but before I was in health I was a muso, like Kurt. I'm too sick to play or write a musical piece for presentations, so I'm sharing instead a piece from a the great jazz pianist Art Tatum and some slides from my final presentation, which I've chosen to call *Critical plays: my body of research.*

(Music starts as slide show of Malcolm's body progresses – it is, literally, his body, as he worsens. He has been photographing, painting, videotaping, and otherwise recording his own death. Lights fade as Jaime watches, mesmerised.

End of play).

ADDITIONAL READING

Ackroyd, J., & O'Toole, J. (2010). *Performing research: Tensions, triumphs and trade-offs of ethnodrama.* Stoke-on-Trent: Trentham Books.

Alexander, B. K. (2005). Performing Ethnography: The re-enacting and inciting of culture. In N. K. Denzin & Y. S. Lincoln (Eds.), *Handbook of qualitative research* (3rd ed., pp. 411-442). Thousand Oaks: Sage Publications, Inc.,

Bagley, C., & Castro-Salazar, R. (2012): Critical arts-based research in education: Performing undocumented historias. *British Educational Research Journal, 38*(2), 239-260.

Barone, T. (1997). "Seen and heard": The place of the child in arts-based research on theatre education. *Youth Theatre Journal, 11*, 113-127.

Barone, T., &d Eisner, E. (1997). Arts based educational research. In R. M. Jaeger (Ed.), *Complementary methods for research in education: A confrontation* (pp. 5-15). Lincoln: University of Nebraska Press.

Belliveau, G., & Lea, G. W. (2). (2011) Research-based theatre in education. In S. Schonmann (Ed.), *Key concepts in theatre drama education* (pp. 332-338). Rotterdam: Sense Publishers.

Bird, J., Donelan, K., Sinclair, C., & Wales, P. (2010). Writing about Alice Hoy. In J. O'Toole & J. Ackroyd (Eds.), *Performing research* (pp. 81-102). London: Continuum Press.

Conquergood, D. (1991). Rethinking ethnography: Towards a critical cultural politics. *Communication Monographs, 58*(3), 179-194.

Conquergood, D. (2002). Performance studies: Interventions and radical research. *The Drama Review, 46*(2) (T174), Summer, 145-156.

Conquergood, D. (2013). *Cultural struggles: Performance, ethnography, praxis.* Ann Arbor: University of Michigan.

Denzin, N. K. (2003). *Performance ethnography: Critical pedagogy and the politics of culture.* Thousand Oaks: Sage Publishers.

Dewey, J. (1934). *Art as experience.* New York: Perigee/Putnam.

Fotheringham, R., Forgasz, R., Ginters, L., Hunter, M., Warrington, L., & Milne, G. (2012). ADS at thirty: Three decades of Australasian drama, theatre, performance and scholarly research. *Australasian Drama Studies*, *60*, 6-19.

Goldstein, T. (2013). *Zero Tolerance and other plays: Disrupting xenophobia, racism and homophobia in schools.* Rotterdam: Sense Publishers.

Greene, M. (1978). Wide-awakeness and the moral life. In M Greene (Ed.), *Landscapes of learning* (pp. 42-52). New York: Teachers College Press.

Harris, A. (2004). Surviving Jonah Salt' (playscript). *From the edge: Two plays from Northern Australia.* Sydney, NSW: Playlab Press.

Harris, A. (2011). Culture Shack and the art of intercultural learning. *Multidisciplinary Research in the Arts*, UNESCO Observatory refereed e-journal.

Harris, A. (2012). *Ethnocinema: Intercultural arts education.* Dordrecht, the Netherlands: Springer SBM.

Harris, A. (2013). Peered and tiered learning: Action research as creative cultural pedagogy. *Educational Action Research*, *21*(3), 412-428. DOI: 10.1080/ 09650792.2013.815046.

Harris, A. (2014). Virtual embodiment as/and the Threshold of Love. *Departures in Critical Qualitative Research*, *3*(2), 97-110.

Harris, A. (2014). *The creative turn: Toward a new aesthetic imaginary.* Rotterdam: Sense Publishers.

Harris, A., & Farrington, D. (2014). 'It gets narrower': Creative strategies for re-broadening queer peer education. *Sex Education: Sexuality, Society and Learning*, *14*(2), 144-158.

Harris, A., & Staley, J. (2011). Schools without walls: creative endeavour and disengaged young people. *Journal of Arts & Creativity in Education* (no pp.).

Hunter, M. (2012). Making the creative process visible. *RealTime Arts*, *110*, 10.

Hunter, M. (2013). Alternative politics of learning: The legacy of TIE in Australia. In A. Jackson & C. Vine (Eds.), *Learning through theatre* (pp. 171-190). London: Routledge.

Hunter, M., & Bourke, L. (2013). A quiet kind of magic: Young people's performance in Australia. In R. Fotheringham & J.Smith (Eds.), *Our Australian theatre in the 2000s* (pp. 123-150). Amsterdam: Rodopi.

Madison, D. S., & Hamera, J. (2006). *The Sage handbook of performance studies.* Thousand Oaks: Sage.

Norris, J. (2009). *Playbuilding as qualitative research: A participatory arts-based approach.* Walnut Creek, CA: Left Coast Press.

Pelias, R. J. (1999). *Writing performance: Poeticizing the researcher's body.* Urbana: Southern Illinois University Press.

Phillips, G. A. (2013). Speaking Barbara Poetry and historical ethnographic fiction. *Qualitative Inquiry, 19*(6), 451-460.

Phillips, G. A. (Forthcoming). He never said anything: A critical poetic response to suicide among young gay men. *Cultural Studies <=> Critical Methodologies.*

Saldaña, J. (2005). *Ethnodrama: An anthology of reality theatre.* Crossroads in Qualitative Inquiry Series, Vol. 5. Walnut Creek, CA: AltaMira Press.

Saldana, J. (2011). *Ethnotheatre: Research from page to stage.* Walnut Creek, CA: Left Coast Press.

Sawyer, R. D., & Norris, J. (2012). *Duoethnography.* London: Oxford University Press.

Sinclair, C. (2000). Rocky talk and the Judas Bull. In J. O'Toole & M. Lepp (Eds.), *Drama for life: Stories of adult learning and empowerment* (pp. 57-66). Brisbane: Playlab Press.

Sinclair, C. (2002). The researcher and the philosopher's stone. *Drama and Learning: Melbourne Studies in Education, 43*(2), 96-107.

Sinclair, C. (2003). Collaborations, creativity and the purpose-built play. *NJ: Drama Australia Journal, 27*(1), 45-54.

Sinclair, C. (2006). A footprint in the mud: entering the engaged space of community theatre practice. *NJ: Drama Australia Journal, 30*(1), 35-46.

Sinclair, C. (2014). 'Return, insistently, to the crossroads': Sites of performance in performed research. In A. Cole & R. Ewing (Eds.), *Performing scholartistry: Arts informed inquiry series.* Backalong Books (in press).

Sinclair, C., & Kelman, D. (2013). Drama, cultural leadership and reflective practice: taking the road to Zamunda. In M. Anderson & J. Dunn (Eds.), *How drama activates learning – Contemporary research and practice* (pp. 28-44). New York & London: Bloomsbury.

Spry, T. (2011). *Body, paper, stage: Writing and performing autoethnography.* Walnut Creek, CA: Left Coast Press.

Wales, P., Sinclair, C., Bird, J., & Donelan, K. (2009). How did you get here? Exploring ethnographic performance. In J. Shu & P. Chan (Eds.), *Planting trees with global vision in local knowledge: IDEA 2007 dialogues* (pp. 490-500). Hong Kong: IDEA Publications.

Wolcott, H. F. (2002). *Sneaky Kid and its aftermath: Ethics and intimacy in fieldwork.* Walnut Creek, CA: Alta Mira Press.

ABOUT THE AUTHORS

Anne Harris, PhD, is a Senior Lecturer in Education at Monash University (Melbourne, Australia), and researches at the intersection of cultural, sexual and gender diversities, including the ways in which creativity, the arts and digital media can be used for social and educational change. She is currently an Australian Research Council 'Discovery Early Career Research Award' (DECRA) Fellow 2014-2016 researching the commodification of creativity, and she was a funded Australian Postgraduate Award scholar (2007-2010, $96,500). Since 2010, Dr Harris has won over $510,000 in competitive research funding, and is a multiple award-winning early career researcher. She earned her PhD from Victoria University (Melbourne) in 2010, using ethnocinema/ethnovideo to collaboratively explore the education experiences of Sudanese young women in Australia. She gained both her MFA and BFA in playwriting/screenwriting from New York University, where she studied with Tony Kushner, Eve Ensler, Wendy Wasserstein, Maria Irene Fornes and Arthur Miller among others. As a playwright, her work has been presented (in NY) at The Public Theatre, Primary Stages, New York Theatre Workshop, Soho Rep, Dixon Place, New Dramatists, Perishable Theatre (RI), Cleveland Public Theatre (OH), and The Playwrights' Centre (MN); and in Australia by Playworks (Sydney), Vitalstatistix and Adelaide Festival Centre (Adelaide), Red Dust Theatre (Alice Springs), JUTE Theatre (Cairns), Darwin Theatre Company and Browns Mart (Darwin), and at the Arts Centre, Melbourne. Anne is a native New Yorker who has also worked professionally as a dramaturg, teaching artist and journalist in the USA and Australia. She is currently co-editor of the journal *Australasian Review of African Studies,* associate editor of the journals *Curriculum and Pedagogy* and *Departures in Critical Qualitative Research*, and on the editorial board of the Palgrave Macmillan book series *Gender and Education* (ed Yvette Taylor, UK), and the Sense Publishers book series *Teaching Writing* (ed Patricia Leavy, USA).

As a scholar, she has published over 50 articles and 6 books on the arts and creativity, culture and diversity, including: *Creativity, Religion and Youth Cultures* (forthcoming Routledge, 2015); *Video as Method* (forthcoming Oxford University Press, 2015); *The Creative Turn: Toward a New Aesthetic Imaginary* (Sense, 2014); *Queer Teachers, Identity and Performativity* (co-ed, Palgrave Macmillan, 2014); *Critical Plays: Embodied Research for Social Change* (Sense, 2014); *South Sudanese Diaspora in Australia and New Zealand: Reconciling the Past with the Present* (co-editor, Cambridge Scholars Press, 2013); and *Ethnocinema: Intercultural Arts Education* (Springer, 2012).

Chris Sinclair is Head of drama education at the University of Melbourne. In addition to teaching in undergraduate and postgraduate programs in teacher education, drama and arts education, she is also a freelance community artist and has written extensively on reflective practitioner research and arts-based research methodologies and community theatre practice. She was a member of a team of researchers who conducted an extended study into ethnographic performance, subsequently producing the play *Alice Hoy is Not a Building*, which was performed at conferences and academic forums in Australia and internationally. In 2014 Chris is convening *Artistry, Performance and Scholarly Inquiry*, an international symposium on the uses of performance in research, to be hosted at The University of Melbourne. This is Chris and Anne's first creative collaboration.

CPSIA information can be obtained at www.ICGtesting.com
Printed in the USA
LVOW04s0100210315

431460LV00003B/154/P